THE STORY OF
MOTHERS &
DAUGHTERS

. . . .

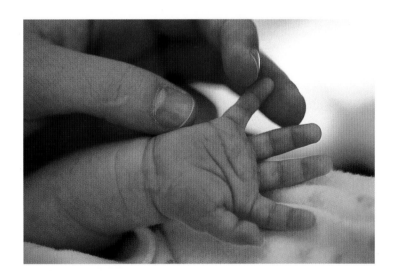

THE STORY OF MOTHERS & DAUGHTERS

BASED ON THE ABC TELEVISION SPECIAL

THE STORY OF MOTHERS & DAUGHTERS

BY JUDITH LEONARD, CATHERINE RYAN, AND GARY WEIMBERG

. . . .

Introduction by Joan Lunden

Director of Photography Peter Howe

Text by Susan Wels

Design by BTD/Beth Tondreau

. . . .

CollinsPublishers

A Division of HarperCollinsPublishers

PHOTOGRAPHY CREDITS

Page i: Lauren Greenfield

Pages ii–iii: Judy Griesedieck

Page iv: Barbara Laing

Pages vi–vii: Nina Barnett

Page viii: Jan Sonnenmair

Page xii: Susie Post

Page xiii: Paul Chesley

Page xiv: Lauren Greenfield

Page xv: Nina Barnett

Page 138: Nina Barnett

Page 142: Lauren Greenfield

Page 144: Joel Sartore

Special thanks to Carole Lee, Gwen Wynn, and Suzanne Regan

Collins books may be purchased for educational, business, or sales promotional use. For information please write: Special Markets Department, HarperCollins Publishers, Inc., 10 East 53rd Street, New York, NY 10022.

FIRST EDITION

Design by BTD/Beth Tondreau, New York, NY

Library of Congress Cataloging-in-Publication Data
The story of mothers & daughters/introduction by Joan Lunden; director of photography, Peter Howe; text by Susan Wels. -1st ed.
        p.   cm.
        "Based on the documentary film The story of mothers & daughters by Judith Leonard, Catherine Ryan, and Gary Weimberg."
        ISBN 0-00-225113-2
        1. Mothers and daughters-United States. 2. Mothers and daughters-United States-Pictorial works. I. Wels Susan. II. Story of mothers & daughters (Motion picture)
        HQ755.85.S76 1997
        306.874'3-dc21   96-37657
Printed in Canada

97 98 99 00 01 /F 10 9 8 7 6 5 4 3 2 1

CONTENTS

Introduction by Joan Lunden • ix

BIRTH • 1

GROWING UP • 23

SEPARATION • 63

WOMAN TO WOMAN • 93

AGING AND RENEWAL • 121

Photographers' Biographies • 139

Acknowledgments • 143

INTRODUCTION

I'll never forget the day I found out I was pregnant for the first time or saw the first ultrasound of my baby. It seemed so surreal. When you realize that there is actually a human being growing inside you, one that you helped create—and will now have to shape into a thinking, feeling person—it's completely overpowering. The cycle of life is intrinsic to nature, something that occurs every day, but there is nothing ordinary about it when it is happening to you—the feeling is awe-inspiring.

And then comes the day you feel your baby moving inside you for the first time. It's exciting, it's a little strange, and it's also a bit scary—for this is the moment when it becomes real. Suddenly, all your fantasies about what your child will be like are replaced by the realities of the responsibility you are about to undertake, and the looming questions about how to nurture and raise this new little person.

Nothing changes your life more than the birth of your first child. One moment, you are an individual free to do whatever you choose. The next, you are a mother. From then on your own needs are secondary. There's nothing that anyone can ever tell you, no book you can read, that prepares you, that accurately reflects the powerful emotions that come with this new link in the cycle of life.

Watching your baby gurgle, smile, laugh, clap, talk, walk, and start to play and think is the most amazing miracle. Motherhood has truly been the most joyous, fulfilling, and important experience of my life. It's also been the most challenging and tiring job I've ever faced . . . and that's saying a lot for someone who has woken up at 4:00 A.M. to go to work for twenty years. (All right, so maybe it was good preparation for those early morning feedings!)

Although motherhood is hard work, constantly requiring you to make tough decisions and set boundaries, I never cease to be amazed at how much my daughters enrich my life. I never knew that macaroni art could elicit such sentiment, or that a finger painting could be as valuable as an original Picasso. My life without my daughters would not only be empty, it would definitely be dull.

The importance of my relationships with my daughters, their impact on my life, and the strength we derive from one another are mirrored in the stories of the women and girls from across the country that appear in *The Story of Mothers & Daughters* documentary and book. These intimate and poignant stories of women and girls from different backgrounds and of different races resonate with me because—although the stories are all unique—they highlight the universal hopes, dreams, and fears all mothers have for their daughters. The stories eloquently describe the many revelations all mothers have as we watch our daughters grow.

One of the most significant of these revelations is recognizing bits and pieces of yourself in your children as they get older. Watching my daughters Jamie, Lindsay, and Sarah is like watching a movie of my life. I hear them speak and I'm taken back in time to when I was their age. I'm sure every parent, for just an instant, has recalled splashing in the tub as they've bathed their child. As I helped my girls learn to ride their bikes, I was reminded of the day I felt those wobbly wheels beneath me. And let's admit it, we buy those doll houses and all those little pieces of furniture because it's just as much fun to play with them the second time around. The difference today is that you can teach your daughter that she can grow up to be the architect of that house.

You also begin to understand just how much your own mother influenced you. You find yourself passing on etiquette—sending thank-you notes, never showing up at someone's house empty-handed—and traditions that establish the importance of family togetherness. As the many mother-daughter stories in the book and documentary make clear, mothers pass on all these important legacies—and have since the beginning of time—and, as the mothers can attest, it's both awesome and exciting to see your passions, desires, attitudes, and dreams reflected in your children. As daughters grow and begin to take on identities of their own, the degree of their mothers' influence becomes more apparent. Just when you think she hasn't been listening to a word you've said, she surprises you by exhibiting the very behavior you had been hoping to pass on.

My mom's influence on my brother and me was enormous. She always wanted us to have a positive attitude, to always try to do the best we could. My mom's name is Gladyce, but it's no accident that her friends all call her Hap, short for Happy. She's always seen the cup as half full, and taught me to approach each day with a smile. Mom tried always to teach us to be fair, to care, and to have integrity. So when I think of these virtues today, I think of my mom.

I also got an incredible sense of confidence from her. She was always her own person. Mom never allowed someone else to shape her convictions. Perhaps the quality that I am most grateful to her for instilling in me is never holding a grudge. It's such a waste of precious time, a drain of energy, and it solves nothing. She believed in kissing and making up, forgiving and forgetting. If we had a disagreement, Mom insisted that we talk about it, get it out, and let it go, and it was never long before she would be at my door with a smile on her face, as if it had never happened. I loved that. I consider that one of the greatest attributes I got from my mom.

Sometimes, it's almost frightening to see how much a mother can shape her daughters. My oldest daughter, Jamie, is very much like me—driven, competitive, hard on herself. She desperately wants to make her mark on life (not to mention save the seals, the rain forests, the world, and everything else). Interestingly, Lindsay reflects different aspects of me. She's nurturing, caring, and the person who sees to it that everyone else is happy and cared for. Sarah embraces the "no limits" concept, and, boy, does she know how to enjoy each moment of the day. She has a great sense of humor, and perhaps because she is the youngest, never lets fear stop her. Her enthusiasm for life is truly contagious.

The profound influence of mothers on their daughters is revealed in each story in this moving film and book. Mothers candidly describe the challenges of raising children and the importance of providing their daughters with the support they need to develop self-confidence. Perhaps most touching, however, are the many mothers who describe their awe at the achievements of their daughters, their daughters' strength and drive and ability to handle, with both grace and resolve, the most stressful situations. Their stories underscore how much mothers learn from their daughters.

The importance of being a good role model is also made clear. If you are a strong enough role model, you can teach the importance of empathy, of putting yourself in the shoes of others less fortunate, and you will create caring, loving adults. And in this society, where unfortunately there seems to be a need to diminish accomplished women, I want my three daughters to always challenge this notion. I want them to have a voice, to believe in themselves, to feel pride in their accomplishments. I want them to think for themselves, to shape their own lives, and to search for their strengths.

My mother always reminded me to reach for the stars and to believe that I could do anything. I have passed on this belief to my girls. By example, I am trying to teach my daughters to find a passion, to make their own choices, and to be willing to take risks. If I can teach them to have confidence in themselves, then they will be able to do anything they think they can do. It's taken me a while to learn this, but that's what finally transforms a daughter into a mother—your years of experience, maturity, wisdom, and the ability to learn from mistakes.

The Story of Mothers & Daughters project is a poignant commemoration of all aspects of mother-daughter relationships—the joys, difficulties, triumphs, challenges, and tragedies experienced along the way. The documentary and book reveal—through the personal stories of the mothers and daughters who participated—the many levels of the mother-daughter connection. Also reflected is the way these bonds change through the course of our lives. This bond is unspoken yet deep, a mystery that can never be explained but one that is understood by every mother and every daughter. Each of the photographs and stories in this book celebrates this intangible yet powerful force.

Joan Lunden

BIRTH

I think my life began with waking up and loving my mother's face.

—GEORGE ELIOT

OPPOSITE:

In Duluth, Georgia, Amy Swarr nuzzles her three-week-old daughter, Elena,
born two months premature. "I feel so much older now, like so much more of a woman,"
says Amy, a 30-year-old C.P.A. "But it's hard. I'm giving, giving, giving all the time.
I just can't wait for Elena to smile back at me."
Photograph by Michael A. Schwarz

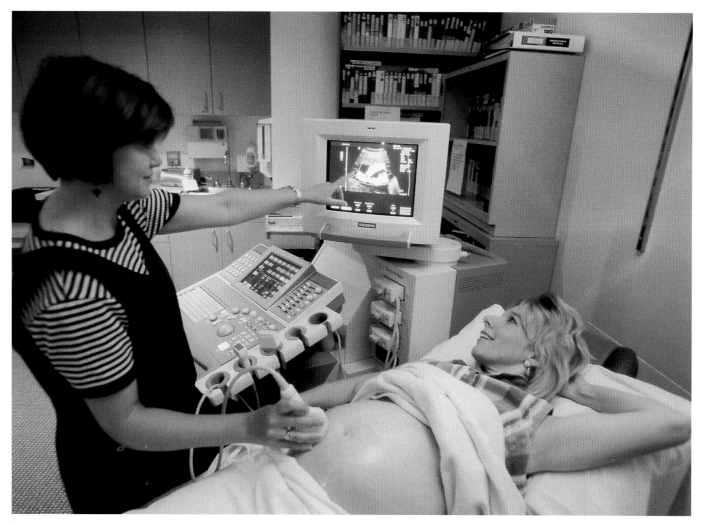

Photograph by Paul Chesley

IT'S A GIRL

Boys are great, but I'm excited about having a girl," exclaims a beaming Rae Johnson-Munoz, 31, upon the discovery that she is having a daughter. Rae, eight months pregnant, watches with anticipation as a doctor points to her unborn baby girl on a monitor during an ultrasound exam. Rae, the mother of two sons, ages five and eight, playfully confesses, "I can't wait to dress her up."

BASIC TRAINING

I t's hard work being a big sister. Six-year-old Kayla Hardenbrook of Denver discovers this in a sibling class taught by Margo McHugh in University Hospital's labor and delivery unit. While her expectant mother, Shannon Hardenbrook, and father, Robert Ott, look on, Kayla studies the fine points of changing a diaper and feeding, burping, and wrapping a new baby—practicing on Margo's good-natured three-month-old Katy—so she'll be ready to help out when her own little brother or sister is born.

Photograph by Paul Chesley

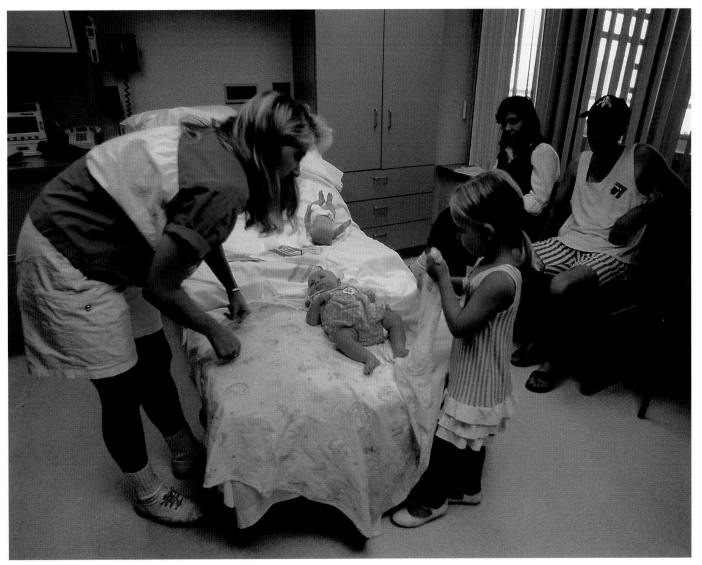

In Chapel Hill, North Carolina, mothers-to-be tone up in an aqua-aerobics class. Gentle water workouts are considered safe for strengthening muscles and loose ligaments. This helps prevent injuries during pregnancy.

Photographs by Annie Griffiths Belt

Photographs by
Lauren Greenfield

SWEET JUSTICE

On a sunny July morning, Justice Yman Gordon emerged into the world strong, healthy, and full-term at Kaiser Sunset Hospital in Los Angeles. Her mother, Felicia Clayton, had spent five anxious months confined to bed after suffering from preterm labor in her fourth month of pregnancy. With two young sons to care for—James, 13, and Kendall, 5—those months in bed were tough. "I don't know how I did it," Felicia says. "I had no job and no money, but I had good friends and family who cleaned my house, cooked my food, and took care of my kids. I had to be positive, because I knew the end result would be a healthy baby."

Things are better now. "Having a girl," she says, "is the most wonderful thing in the world. I'll be able to share all of the things I love with her, put barrettes in her hair, and dress her in those wonderful little clothes." Felicia, who is studying toward a master's degree in criminal justice and planning to enter law school in 1997, named her daughter Justice as a reminder of her own interests and commitment. "More than anything," she says, "I want her to know that she can achieve anything she wants on this earth—and I hope her name will give her something to stand for."

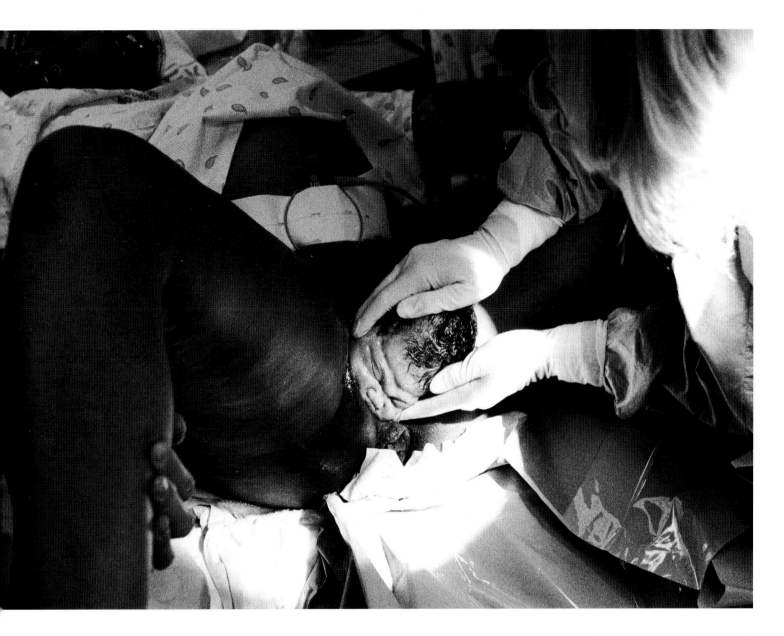

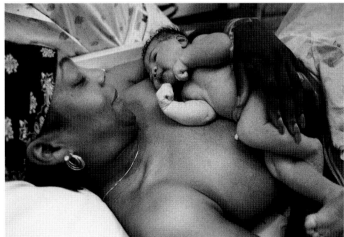

WARM WELCOME

In Corona, California, midwives check Lisa Kahan's progress as she prepares to deliver her first child in a birthing tub at home, in the arms of her husband, Geoff. Water births can be soothing for the mother and, practitioners believe, provide an easier transition for the newborn, who moves from the womb's amniotic fluid into the watery environment of the tub. Just before 3:00 P.M., after more than 40 hours of labor, the Kahans' baby daughter, Rachel Joy, slipped out into the warm water and into the midwife's waiting hands.

Photograph by Lee Celano

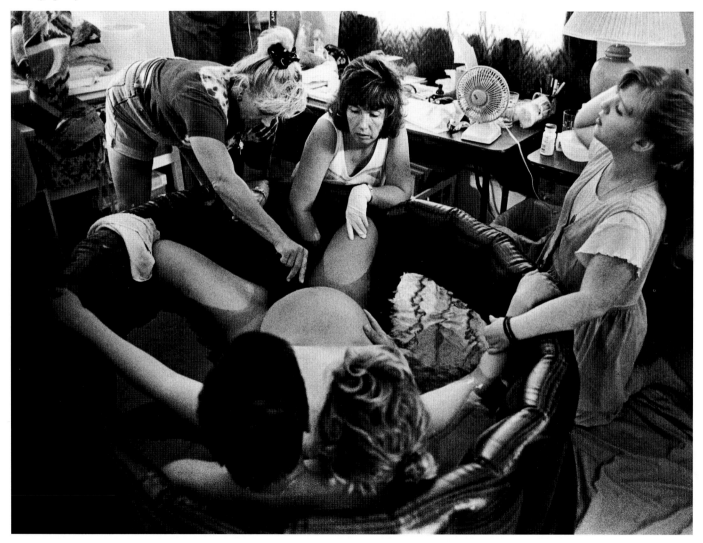

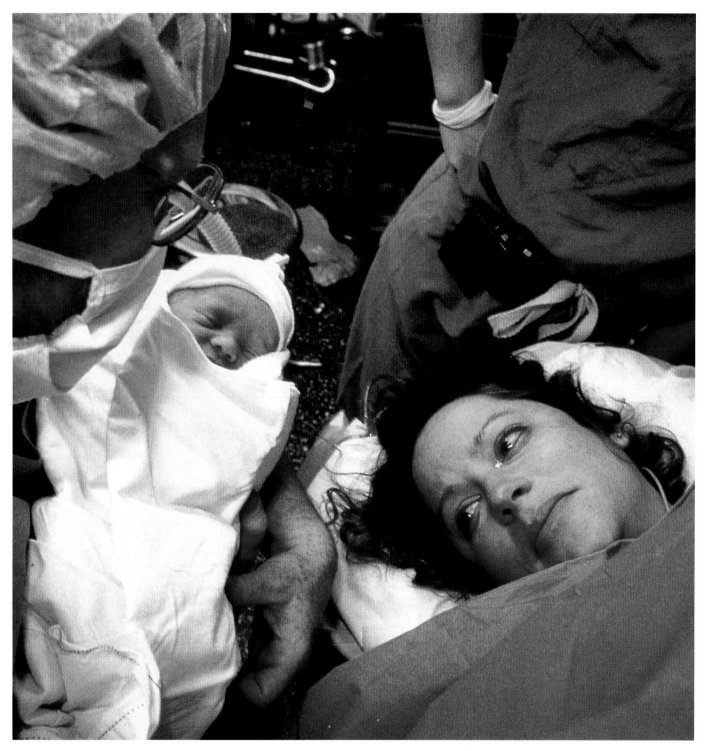

Photograph by Annie Griffiths Belt

THREE AT ONCE

Lisa Gilbert gazes at her newborn daughter, one of three infants she gave birth to that day by cesarean section at Johns Hopkins Medical Center in Baltimore. The triplets—Hayley, Emma, and a boy, Connor—all came into the world within four minutes. Lisa is also the mother of Taylor, six, "the most incredible big brother in the world."

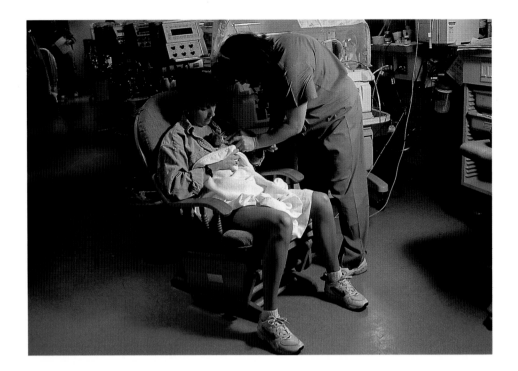

Photographs by Judy Griesedieck

SKIN TO SKIN

At St. Paul Children's Hospital in St. Paul, Minnesota, Jill Wurm nestles and warms her fragile three-week-old daughter, Lindsey, against her bare skin. Lindsey, born almost four months early, weighed only one pound twelve ounces at birth. Twice each day, Jill travels half an hour from her home in Afton to the hospital, where she holds her tiny baby, skin-to-skin, for as long as two hours at a time. "When Lindsey is out of the incubator and in my arms, she can smell my skin and feel my heartbeat," Jill explains. The closeness helps them bond, despite the feeding tube and bulky ventilator that pumps oxygen into Lindsey's undeveloped lungs. The first time Jill ever held her daughter, the day after she was born, she remembers that she could fit her baby's entire body in her hands. "She felt like a little bird," Jill recalls. "I cried the whole time." Her daughter's long stay in the hospital has been hard. "When something goes right for Lindsey, something else usually goes wrong. It's been one step forward, two steps back, since she was born. But in some ways it's been positive. It's made me grow up fast. I just stay focused on the fact that things could always be worse."

HOLDING ON *(overleaf)*

Lorie Hurne grasps the tiny hand of her two-day-old daughter, Amber Rene. Born two months early and weighing only two pounds twelve ounces, Amber stayed for more than a month in the neonatal intensive care unit at Denver's University Hospital.

OVERLEAF:
Photograph by Paul Chesley

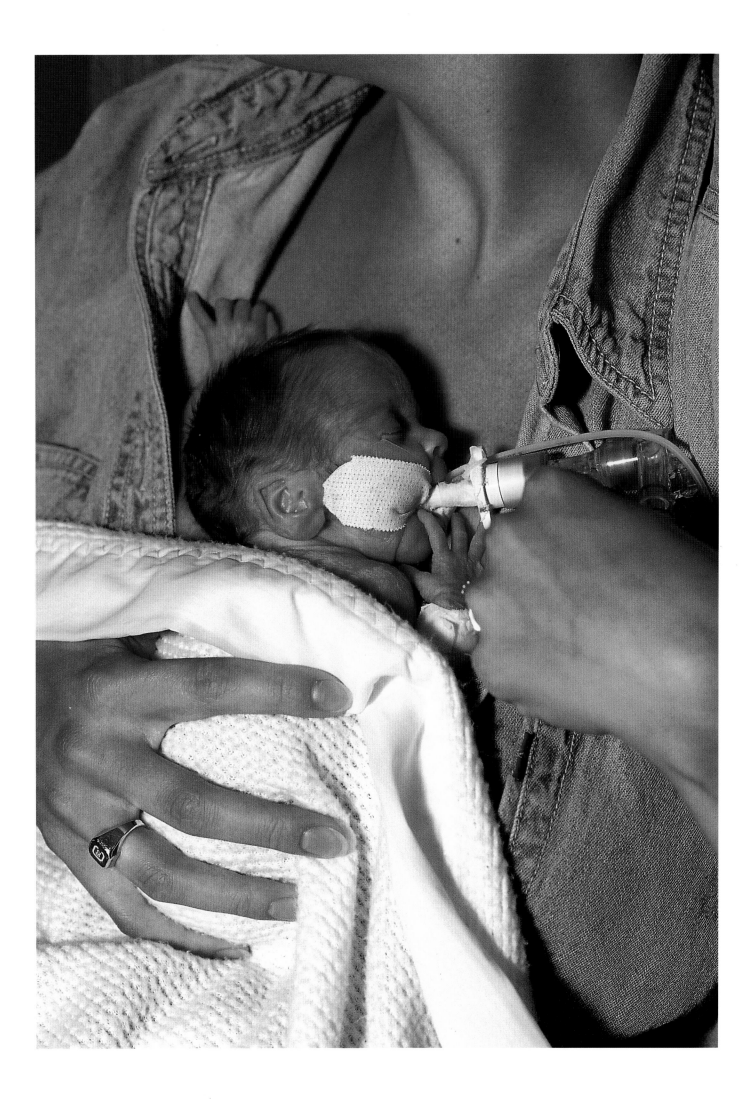

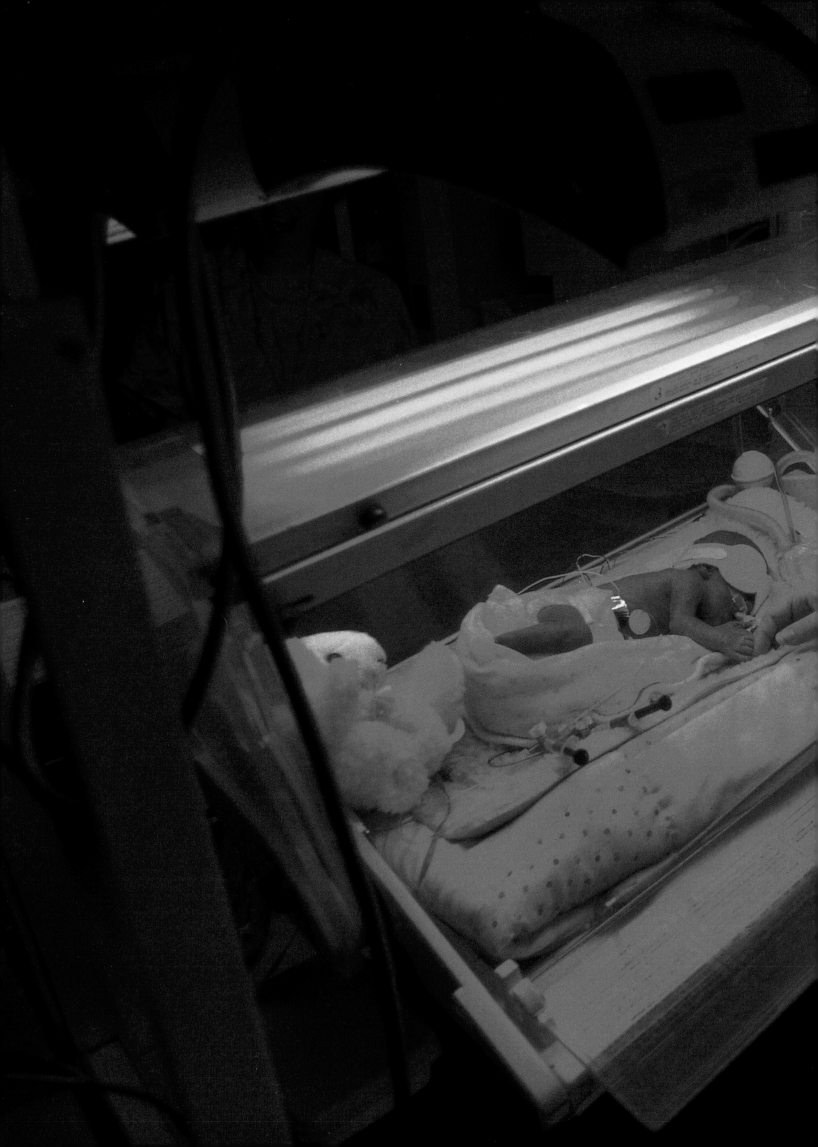

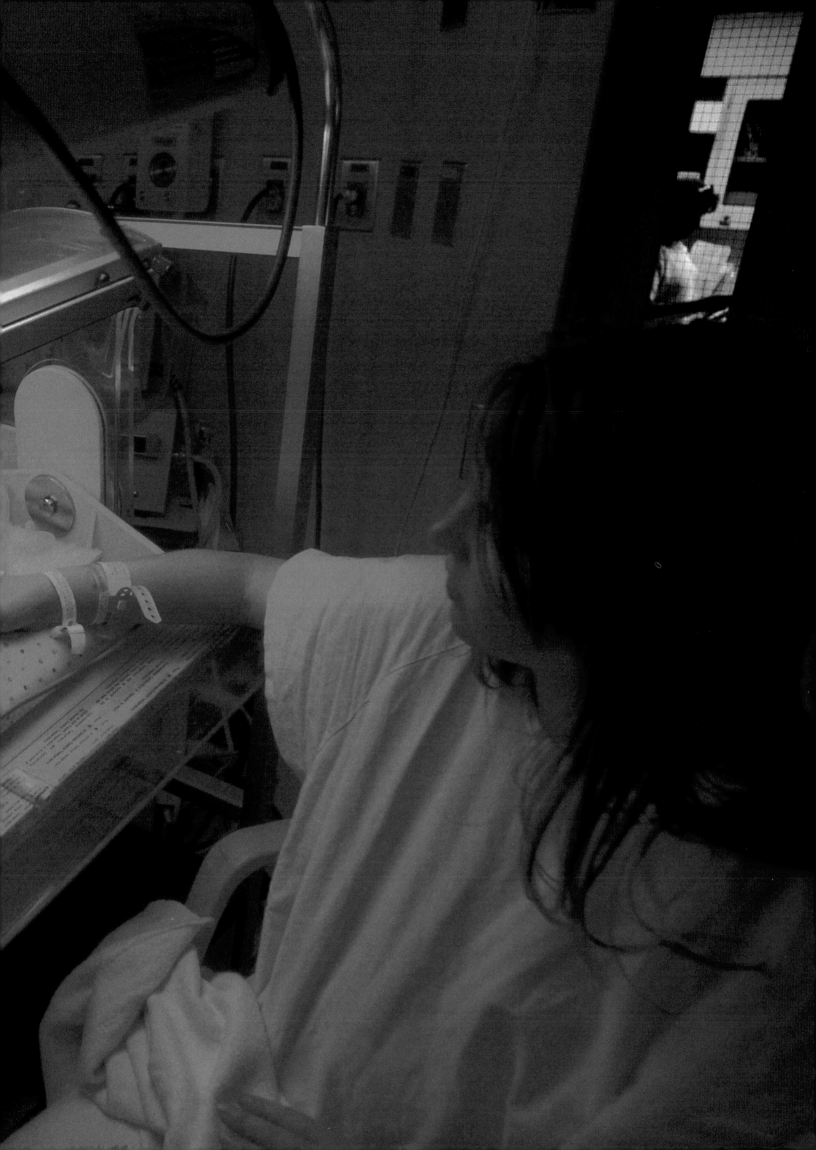

Photographs by
Lauren Greenfield

A DELICATE BALANCE

With help from a temporary baby nurse, Tracey Roberts, 33, passes her days at home in the Hollywood Hills in a fatiguing cycle of feeding, holding, and comforting her somewhat colicky six-week-old daughter, Sophie Haigney. "It's been a really challenging time," admits Tracey, formerly an interior decorator and now a full-time mother. "I love having Sophie—she's amazingly bright. But sometimes keeping her happy and myself sane is a kind of delicate balance."

Photographs by Judy Griesedieck

DOUBLE LOVE

Two baby girls are lots more fun than one, according to Trish Gardiner, 38, of Apple Valley, Minnesota. "I can't imagine life without twins. It would be lonely," insists the mother of eight-week-old handfuls Kara (left) and Maya. No matter how chaotic life gets, she adds, "nothing compares with seeing four eyes and two big smiles focused on me first thing every morning."

Trish, a conflict-resolution trainer, has an older daughter too—Danica, age nine—as well as an 18-year-old son. Since the twins were born, Trish has made a point of spending special time alone with Danica—going out to dinner and on bike rides—to help her adjust to the sudden arrival of her sisters. "Our relationship has moved up to a different level since the girls were born," Trish acknowledges. "Now that she has baby sisters, Danica's grown up a lot. But even though she's over five feet tall, she still sometimes climbs on my lap and wants me to rock her like a baby. No matter how big she seems, she's still a little girl inside."

PLAYING IT SAFE

For Laura Medina, a waitress in Las Vegas, having a baby daughter has totally changed her priorities and thinking about life. "Alyssa comes first now, no matter what," says the 21-year-old single mother. This means that some lifelong dreams, like going sky diving, are out of the question, at least for now. "I won't even consider doing something that risky," Laura says. "I'm afraid of doing anything that means I might not be here to raise my daughter."

Photograph by
Lauren Greenfield

Photograph by Paul Chesley

WATCHING THE WORLD

In Browning, Montana, Mona Nordwall carries her six-week-old baby daughter, Tonantzin (Earth Mother), in a traditional Shoshone cradleboard. The stiff swaddling, made of willow and canvas, holds the baby's arms and legs, eliminating distracting movements so that her little daughter can focus on observing the world around her and sharpening her mind.

STROLLER DERBY

Every Friday morning in Santa Monica, California, some 15 moms and babies rendezvous at the Coffee Bean and Tea Leaf Cafe, then head out for a two-hour group stroll around the beach. "We talk about kids, sex, work, politics—everything," says Karen Rappaport McHugh (left), who, with her daughter, Aliza Jane, has been a regular since the stroller group started in early 1996. "It's something we do for exercise, for companionship, and for the kids."

RIGHT AND FOLLOWING PAGES:
Aliza Jane McHugh, nine months, samples the sea air at Santa Monica Beach.
Photographs by Jan Sonnenmair

GROWING UP

Who ran to help me when I fell,

And would some pretty story tell,

Or kiss the place to make it well?

My mother.

—ANN TAYLOR, "My Mother," *Original Poems for Infant Minds*

Photograph by
Lauren Greenfield

FIRST HOLY COMMUNION

Pat Donnelly helps her eight-year-old daughter Erin with finishing touches before her first holy communion at Saint Claire's Church in Canyon Country, California. Pat, a nurse-midwife, sees the ceremony as the passing on of a religious tradition as well as a rite of passage for her daughter. "I want to give all three of my girls a sense of the values and religious background I grew up with," Pat says. "They'll have a foundation. Then, when they're older, they can make their own choices."

HOME TEAM

Maura Cameron's four-year-old triplets—two daughters, Brenna and Caitlin, and a son, Pierce—are totally devoted to one another. "If one of them is missing for five minutes," she says, "the other two are devastated. They always talk about themselves as 'we.'"

Even though the triplets share a birthday and are raised in exactly the same way, there are classic differences between the two girls and their brother, according to Maura, a part-time obstetrics nurse in Littleton, Colorado. "Brenna and Caitlin," she observes, "are a lot more into playing, feelings, and relationships. And even though it's the nineties," she adds, "the girls are somehow getting the idea from school and TV that only boys grow up to be doctors, astronauts, and police officers. It's important for me to keep stressing to my daughters that they can be whatever they want to be."

Photograph by Mary Ellen Mark

FUTURE FOCUS

Mary Ann Ramirez, 18, poses with her daughter, Victoria, in her hometown of Sunnyside in the rural Yakima Valley—a hub of drug trafficking, gangs, and violent crime in Washington state. Victoria was born in Texas, where Mary Ann had been living at the time with her older sister. A single mother, Mary Ann hopes to go back to school someday to become a psychotherapist or prison guard.

Photograph by Mary Ellen Mark

RIDING HIGH

Horseback riding is a shared passion of Libby Edelman, 42, and her ten-year-old daughter, Callie. The two of them spend a lot of time riding together on the family's working horse farm in Westchester, New York, and traveling to horse shows to compete in jumping. "Callie and I are like twins," says Libby. "We look alike, do so many of the same things, and have a lot of the same attitudes."

Photograph by
Lauren Greenfield

FUN FOR TWO

Brittany Egger, seven, carries the flag in the Fourth of July parade in Kailua on the island of Oahu. She and her mother, Tracy, moved to Hawaii from Los Angeles in 1994, and they haven't looked back since. In addition to frequent sand-castle-building sessions at the beach, the two of them have discovered the joys of baton tossing, taking weekly classes together at the nearby Tropical Twirling School.

Photographs by Paul Chesley

EASY RIDERS

Winning comes easily to Sadie Johnson and her little sister, Shanna. At ages 12 and 10, the girls have already made names for themselves as top competitors on the rodeo circuit from Montana to Canada. Their skill is barrel racing—running trained horses around three barrels in a cloverleaf pattern. The fastest time wins, and the sisters have ridden off with more than their share of buckles, saddles, and cash prizes since they started competing at the ages of three and four. "They're naturals," says their mother, Robin, 33, who has been a rodeo rider herself since she was 10. "I get more of a thrill out of watching my daughters compete than I ever did when I raced." The girls, she explains, were practically born in the saddle on the family's vast cattle ranch in Browning, Montana. "They help with whatever has to be done," she adds—from grazing, branding, and shipping out the cattle to putting up hay and helping with the calving in the spring. Natural competitors, Sadie and Shanna have also been eager to take their chances in beauty queen contests. Shanna was named first runner-up in the Northwest Montana State Fair Rodeo Queen Contest, and Sadie has traveled to Orange County, California, as a Miss Junior America contestant.

ABOVE: *Robin Johnson and her daughters, Shanna (left) and Sadie, relax by the general store in West Glacier Park, Montana, near their cattle ranch.*

FOLLOWING PAGES: *At sunset, the girls and their mother ride out on the land that has been in their family for five generations.*

Photographs by
Lauren Greenfield

PERFECT PARTNERS

Togetherness is happiness for Kate O'Neal and her daughter, Soleil, five. "She's my best buddy," says Kate, a professional fund-raiser in Los Angeles. It's just been the two of them together for the four and a half years since Kate and Soleil's father divorced. They sleep in the same bed, and every Friday night, without fail, the two of them go dancing or bike a mile down the beach to the Santa Monica Pier. Being Soleil's mother has been a revelation to the career-oriented Kate, who had always expected that having a child would be more work than fun. "My daughter has brought out nurturing qualities in me that I never knew I had."

Photographs by Barbara Laing

STRONG SUPPORT

From the living room couch, where she spends long hours when she's ill, Rebecca Cowell, ten, gazes out past the Fourth of July flags strung from her back porch in Stillwater, Oklahoma. A few days after Christmas in 1995, Rebecca was diagnosed with Ewing's sarcoma, a malignant, inoperable tumor in her pelvic bone. Since then, she has been on an aggressive treatment of radiation and chemotherapy at Children's Hospital in Oklahoma City, an hour's drive away. Rebecca spends one week in the hospital for chemotherapy, then two weeks at home recovering. Her mother, Annette, is always by her side, checking to be sure that her daughter takes her medicines and makes her bed, teaching her when she's not well enough to go to school, and sleeping in a folding chair at her bedside in the hospital. "We've both learned what we can survive with," Annette says. "I've taken a lot of time off from work to take care of Rebecca, but the world hasn't ended. On good days, when she's feeling well and her counts are good, I think, 'This isn't so bad.'" She adds, "Rebecca has lost her hair, but that's not really a big deal either. She's still beautiful without it."

LEFT: *The day before Rebecca goes back to the hospital for chemotherapy, her mother, Annette, draws her blood at home. They always keep the blood sampling equipment on the same paper plate, which Rebecca has decorated with the words "I Love You" for her mom.*

BELOW: *Rebecca and Annette watch television in the Children's Hospital pediatric oncology waiting area until a room becomes available.*

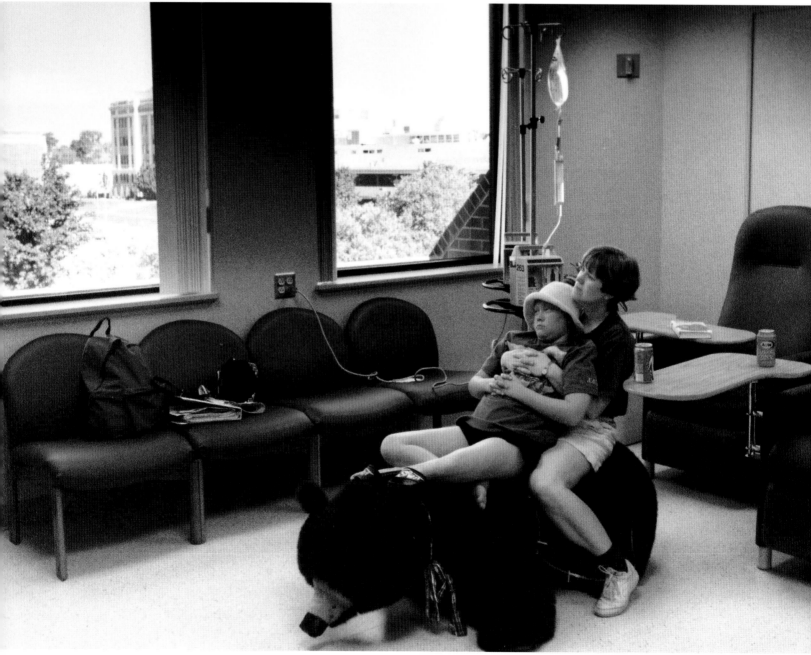

ABOVE: *When Rebecca feels weak and very sick, especially the first days after treatment, she spends a lot of time with her favorite pillow on the living room couch.*

FOLLOWING PAGES: *Mother and daughter spend time resting and relaxing.*

Photograph by Paul Chesley

TINY DANCER

All decked out in buckskin, 20-month-old Shayni Fontenelle draws admiring looks at the annual Blackfeet powwow in Browning, Montana. Shayni—half Zuni and half Northern Arapaho—is already a competitive dancer and has traveled from Zuni, New Mexico, with her family to perform in the powwow's Tiny Tots division. Her mother, Cassie SoldierWolf, competes in Northern Women's Traditional Dancing.

WATER MUSIC

Mapuana deSilva and her daughters, Kahikina (left), 19, and Kapalai'ula (center), 12, perform a chant and hula on Lanikai Beach, near their home on the Hawaiian island of Oahu. Mapuana, a master teacher, has taught hula to thousands of men and women at her renowned school, Halau Mohala Ilima, and has inspired her daughters to become serious students of the dance. Both girls began studying hula at age five, and Kahikina will be officially recognized as an *olapa*, or dancer, when she turns 20.

Photograph by Lauren Greenfield

Photographs by Mary Ellen Mark

DAY BY DAY

Pam Cowan can't think about the future. Her present is too demanding, and the years ahead of her are too uncertain to imagine. Her focus is on the minute-to-minute needs and comfort of her daughter, Rebecca, who, at age four, is unable to sit, talk, or hold her own head up. When she was born, the doctors knew there was something very wrong—but they were, and are, unable to explain her low muscle tone or the frequent seizures that she has suffered since birth. Pam, a former oncology nurse, cares for Rebecca and her two-year-old brother, Zachary, at home in Wilton, Connecticut. She tries, she says, to take things day by day. "As Rebecca's gotten older, she seems to suffer more. That's the hardest part," Pam admits. "I agonize about my daughter and her comfort. But Rebecca's such a joy to us, despite everything she's gone through. When my husband or I am at our wits' end, she somehow always rallies. It's her smile that pulls us through."

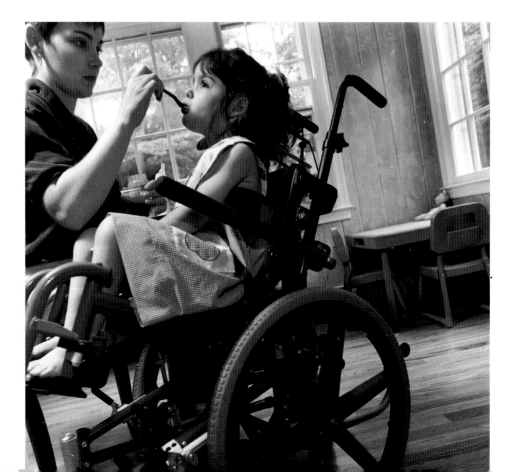

DEEP TIES

Lily Cohen's relationship with her mother, Karen Sukoneck, has been marked by a deep mother-daughter bond. Karen, a divorced mom, was diagnosed with multiple sclerosis eleven years ago when Lily was five. The two lived together in Sag Harbor, supported by Karen's freelance graphic design work, until 1995. It was at this time that Karen could no longer maintain her business because of the progression of the disease. Lily enrolled in a Connecticut boarding school while her mother moved to New York to live with relatives. "I miss her," Karen says, "but think it's wonderful for her to be away at school. She's always been so helpful and kind, but now she's gained so much maturity. She amazes me."

Photograph by Mary Ellen Mark

RIGHT: *Ann and Alicia Daugherty start the day by braiding each other's hair and playing with baby Luke.*
Photographs by Barbara Laing

HOME SCHEMOOL

HOME SCHOOL

Being a wife and mother means being a lot of things to a lot of people," says Ann Daugherty, mother of Alicia, eight, and sons Asa, four, and Luke, nine months. She and her family live on a working cattle ranch at the end of a rough dirt road in west Texas. Because they are more than 50 miles away from the nearest schools, Ann and her husband have chosen to teach their children at home. After schoolwork is finished in the morning, Alicia helps her mom with household chores and pitches in to run their ranch—branding and vaccinating the cattle and working with them on horseback. In case of an emergency, the Daughertys have also taught Alicia how to drive the family's car. "We're so far away from the highway that we thought it would be a good idea to teach Alicia to drive in case of an emergency," Ann explains.

LEFT: *In the ranch schoolroom, Ann struggles to keep Alicia focused on a spelling test.*

BELOW: *Ann and Alicia cuddle with the kittens in the barn.*

TOP AND ABOVE LEFT: *Ann and her daughter often ride together on their west Texas cattle ranch.* ABOVE RIGHT: *Ann has Alicia practice driving the family car in case she ever needs to get help.* OPPOSITE: *Mother and daughter spend a few quiet moments together before supper.*

FIGHT FOR LIFE

Cynthia Galvez had led a happy, ordinary life. She was starting second grade at St. Gertrude School in Bell Gardens, California, and had just celebrated her seventh birthday when she was diagnosed suddenly with leukemia. For two months, she traded Barbie dolls, school, and play dates for daily ten-hour chemotherapy treatments at Children's Hospital in Los Angeles, California. "She never complained about it," says her mother, Anna. "She knew she had a bad disease and had to take the medications. But she was a fighter. The chemo never even made her very sick." She and her mother got good news a few months later— Cynthia was in remission. For two years, the family returned to normal life. "Cynthia was back at school, swimming, and playing with friends," Anna remembers. "We all put the illness aside and really believed that it was over." Then, in November 1995, Cynthia's leukemia came back. Anna quit her job in hospital management to be with her daughter full-time as she battled through months of chemotherapy and a rare fungal infection. But by July 1996 the doctors knew that the chemotherapy wasn't working. A bone marrow transplant was their last hope, but the only donor they found had disappeared. Anna knew then that Cynthia would die. "I think Cynthia knew too, but she was scared to leave us," Anna says. "She fought really hard to get better. She was so strong, and she always kept smiling, even though she was in pain. She didn't want to discuss it, but we told her about heaven and that it was okay to let go." Cynthia passed away on August 12.

RIGHT: *Anna Galvez comforts her ten-year-old daughter, Cynthia, during a bad day at Children's Hospital in Los Angeles.*

OPPOSITE: *A good sport, Cynthia posed in her frilly ninth-birthday outfit, despite the fact that she hated wearing dresses.*
Photographs by Mary Ellen Mark

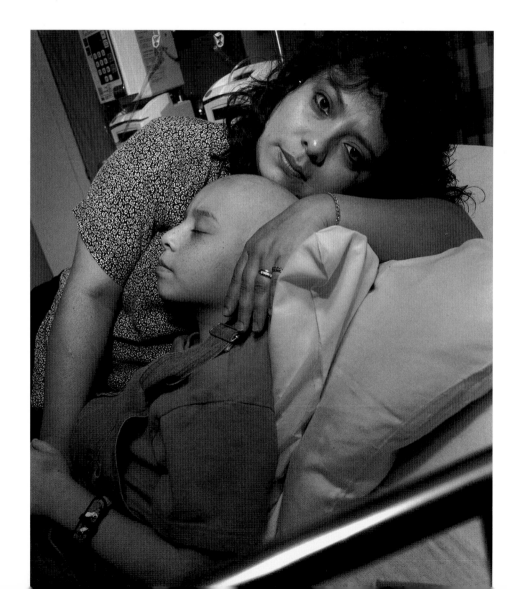

ABOVE: *On a summer afternoon, Rolla Crandall makes pesto from basil she's harvested with her daughters (left to right) Diana, Jessica, Shayna, and Rochelle.* Photograph by Judy Griesedieck

LABOR OF LOVE

Rolla Crandall's passion is bringing children into the world. A midwife in Brooklyn Park, Minnesota, Rolla, 36, has delivered 130 babies over the past 10 years. She has also borne four daughters of her own—Jessica, 12, Rochelle, 9, Diana, 7, and Shayna, 4—and is expecting her fifth child. Jessica watched her sister Rochelle come into the world, and the two older girls helped their mother through labor when the third child, Diana, was born. "They're all really excited about being there when the new baby arrives," Rolla says, "but birth is still a very emotional and intimate experience for me. I may just let the girls sleep."

DREAM TEAM

Linda Pendleton and her daughters have a dream, and they're going after it together. Linda, a 35-year-old private-duty nurse in South Central Los Angeles, hopes to open an inn and supper club near Barstow, California. Her younger daughter Melody, 17, just completed a Job Corps course in culinary arts and plans to train so that she can be the chef. Linda's older daughter Tamita, 21— "a brilliant kid," her mother says, who graduated from high school at age 14—will be the business manager. "She's the brains of the family," Linda declares. Tamita says she shares her mother's goal. "My mom has a lot of ideas and a big heart, and she's always come through for us," Tamita says. "I hope that when she's ready to pull this off, I have the knowledge and training I need to help her."

LEFT: *In their South Central Los Angeles apartment, Linda Pendleton watches her older daughter Tamita fix her sister's hair.*
Photograph by Lauren Greenfield

FOLLOWING PAGES: *Nancy Montgomery drives her daughters, Erin (left) and Mary, down a country road near their ranch in Bennett, Nebraska.*
Photograph by Joel Sartore

COUNTRY LIVING

A fishing pond, a pool, wide open spaces for exploring—in Nancy Montgomery's opinion, rural Nebraska is the best possible place to raise two daughters. Nancy and her husband, Don, produce 10,000 white Landrace pigs a year on their 80-acre hog ranch, Fine Swine Farms, near Bennett. Everyone in the family, including Erin, 15, and Mary, 13, helps out. The girls feed the pigs and trim teeth and tails. Except for the overwhelming smell of hogs—which Erin says is something you get used to—they like everything about farm life, especially the privacy, quiet, and their time together as a family. Although Nancy works with the hogs a quarter mile away from the house, the girls appreciate the fact that they can always run up to see her if they need to. "It's fun being with the animals," Mary says, "and having your parents close."

BELOW: *Working on the family farm, Nancy keeps an eye on her daughters.* Photographs by Joel Sartore

ABOVE: *Helping hands: Mary, Nancy, and Erin Montgomery*

FOLLOWING PAGES: *In between chores, such as vaccinating one- to three-day-old piglets, the girls relax in the back of the family pickup and on the tractor with their mom.*

*The Montgomery family raises geneti-
cally improved breeding stock to sell
to other farmers. Erin has honed her
own swine-raising skills and has won
four blue ribbons showing hogs at
county and state fairs.*

ABOVE: *Mary and Erin take a nap after finishing their chores.*

FOLLOWING PAGES: *Jody Proctor (kneeling, second from right) started the Greencastle Softball Club to give 8- to 18-year-old girls in Greencastle, Indiana—including her 14-year-old daughter Jessica (first row, second from right)—the chance to play fast-pitch softball at the regional and state levels. In 1996, its second year, the club had a 50-50 record against rival fast-pitch teams in Brazil, Crawfordsville, and Coverdale.* Photograph by Dan Dry

SEPARATION

R esign yourself to the fact that, from the time your daughter is 12 until she's 18, whatever you do will be wrong.

—MOTHER OF THREE

Photographs by Barbara Laing

ABOVE: *Preschooler Carly Tull, four, holds on tight to her mom on her first day at Trinity School.*

RIGHT: *Suzanne Sura spends a few minutes in the kindergarten class with her five-year-old daughter, Gloria.*

FIRST DAY

Some preschoolers and kindergarteners have a harder time letting go of their mothers than others. In Midland, Texas, five-year-old Gloria Sura (above right) couldn't wait for her first three-hour day of kindergarten at Trinity School. "She loves it," says her mother, Suzanne. "She'd go all day if she could." Four-year-old Carly Tull (top left), on the other hand, wasn't as enthusiastic about her first day at preschool. "Her legs were pretty stiff when she was walking—I don't think she wanted to go," comments her mother, Marcy. To help her daughter feel a little more secure, Marcy tucked Carly's favorite stuffed animal in her school bag.

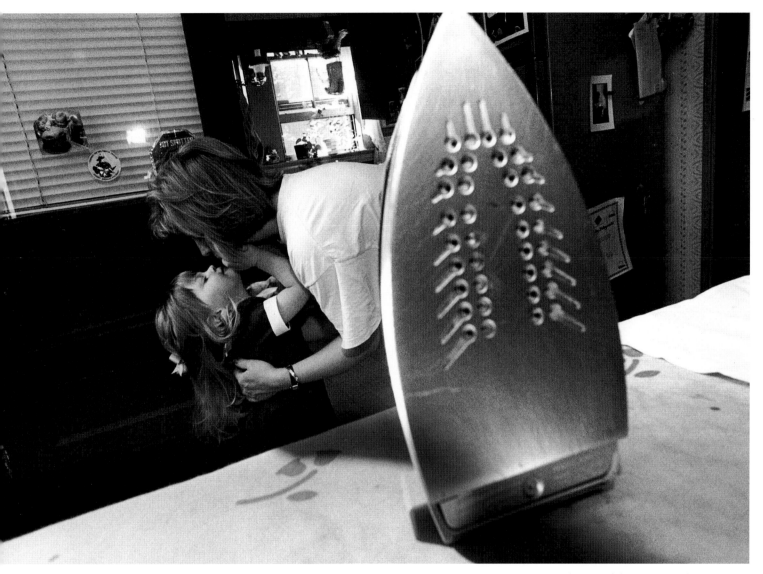

Photograph by Eugene Richards/
Magnum Photos, Inc.

PRESSED FOR TIME

Before rushing off to work and daycare in Stoughton, Massachusetts, Lynn Fitzgerald interrupts her ironing to get a hug from daughter Meghan.

ABOVE: *At Pinemere Camp in the Poconos, Sallie Stutz lingers over a game of Ping-Pong, then gives her daughter, Julia, a bear hug before saying good-bye and leaving her for two months at summer camp.*

RIGHT: *Sharon Etter (right) reconnects with her 12-year-old daughter Lindsay on parents' visiting day.*
Photographs by Scott Thode

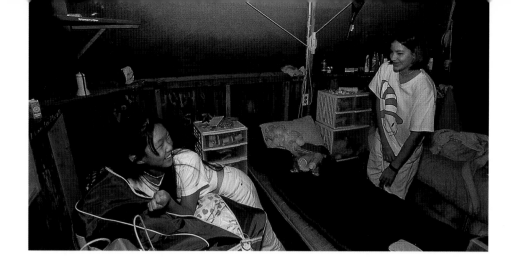

SUMMER BREAK

For three generations of kids, a summer away from home at Pinemere Camp in Pennsylvania's Pocono Mountains has meant a taste of independence along with plenty of fresh air. At age 12, Katie Holden from Cherry Hill, New Jersey, has already spent seven summers at the coed camp, founded in 1942. "I like being away from my parents for a while," Katie says. "Even though I'm sad when they leave me here, I'm always excited to see my friends, and by now I'm used to being away from my mom and dad." A month or two of separation can be a break for parents, too. Sallie Stutz's eight-year-old daughter, Julia, has spent two summers at Pinemere. "I miss her when she's gone, but I love knowing that she's having a great time," says Sallie, who works for the Brooklyn Museum in New York City. "When Julia's gone, life is definitely more relaxing and spontaneous—my husband and I can decide to go to a movie at midnight or have a drink together after work. I'm not worried about fixing dinner or making sure all the homework gets done. It's a nice break—but by the end of the summer, I'm ready to get her back."

ABOVE AND BELOW:
Lauren Glazerman (above left) and Katie Holden pack up to go home on their last night at Pinemere. During their summer at sleepaway camp, they formed close friendships with bunkmates Joanna Katz (below left) and Abby Neff (below, second from left).

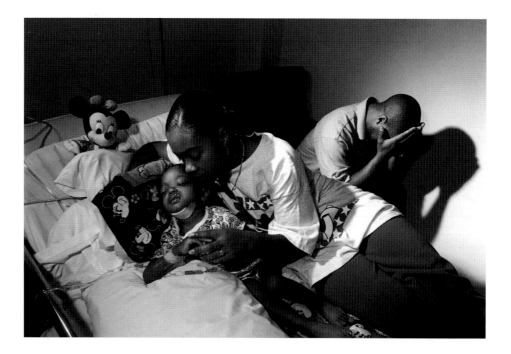

Photographs by Mary Ellen Mark

ABOVE: *Two-year-old Keilanie Quinn is surrounded by her parents' love and grief during her last week of life at Children's Hospital in Los Angeles.*

OPPOSITE: *Keiana Quinn lets go of her daughter. "No matter what," she says, "I will always be her mom."*

A LITTLE TIME

Keilanie Quinn was only 18 months old when she was diagnosed with a virulent form of leukemia in March 1995. After a year of aggressive chemotherapy at Children's Hospital in Los Angeles, the doctors told her mother, Keiana, that the treatment wasn't working. A bone-marrow transplant might have given her a slight chance of survival, but Keiana decided against the risky and devastating procedure. "If Keilanie had undergone the transplant, she would have been in isolation for up to six months," Keiana explains. "She might have passed away, and I wouldn't have been able to hold her." Instead, Keiana took her daughter off chemotherapy and brought her home. For the next three months, Keilanie lived like a happy two-year-old. "For the first time, she went running through the mall," Keiana remembers. "She went to Disneyland, Universal Studios, and Knott's Berry Farm. We had our first real Christmas, where I cooked dinner and she opened presents at home." The Make-A-Wish Foundation even gave her a special third birthday party, two months early, at Bullwinkle's Family Fun Center. Soon after, however, Keilanie's health deteriorated. Weak and very ill, she returned to the hospital, where her mother and the nursing staff struggled for two more months to keep her comfortable. "I lay with her in bed all day, every day, while she watched videos," Keiana recalls. Family members constantly came to visit. Then, on July 12 at two in the morning, Keilanie passed away. "The night before she died, she told me she had seen angels," Keiana says. "She said that they were nice and that she was ready to go with them. My baby was so adorable and brave. I thank the Lord for every day that she was with me."

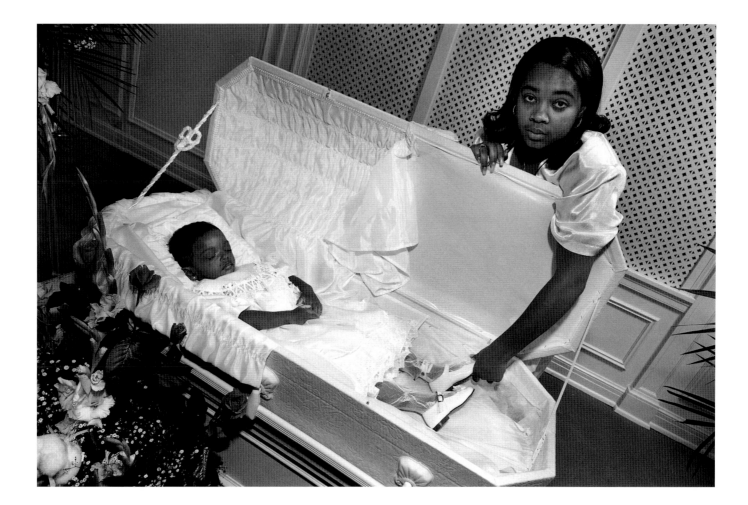

ABOVE: *Graduating seniors at Cornelia Connelly School of the Holy Child finish last-minute preparations before the commencement ceremony begins.*
Photographs by Lauren Greenfield

NEW BEGINNINGS

For most of the young women graduating from Cornelia Connelly School of the Holy Child in Anaheim, California, commencement is a beginning—of adulthood, independence, and discovery of the endless possibilities of life. For their mothers, it is a bittersweet day. They are proud, yet also realize that their relationships with their daughters will change as they move beyond the familiar roles of childhood to forge new connections, woman to woman.

ABOVE AND FOLLOWING PAGES: *Connelly graduates pose for their last pictures together.*

ABOVE AND OPPOSITE: *High school graduation is an emotional, proud day for mothers and daughters at Cornelia Connelly School.*

TOUGH LOVE

It's been an uphill climb for Alexa Baehr, 15, and her mother, Allyn, who has raised her daughter alone for 12 years. Strong-willed, Alexa has been a parenting challenge from the start. Her defiance and destructive behavior became unmanageable as she reached puberty and her mother filed for alternative housing placement when she was 14. Alexa refused the new placement and lived in Seattle youth shelters and on the streets. She began attending an alternative summer school where a group was formed to help homeless youth. Peace for the Streets by Kids from the Streets organizes benefit rock concerts to help support homeless youth shelters. Alexa and her mother are now working through their problems together and Alexa is working toward a fresh start through an independent living program.

ABOVE AND RIGHT: *According to Allyn Baehr, her daughter, Alexa, was always a handful as a child.*
Photographs by Susie Fitzhugh

SEARCH FOR PEACE

Anger and pain, in almost equal measure, fill the days of Debra Glenn and her 14-year-old daughter, Martha. An honor student at Christ Crusader Academy in Harlem, Martha became suddenly and inexplicably ill in 1993. At first, when emergency room doctors informed Debra that her daughter might have HIV, she thought the diagnosis was impossible. Then she remembered that a few days after her daughter's premature birth in May 1982, she had seen a little red bag by Martha's incubator in the hospital. Without her knowledge, her baby had been given a transfusion. Eleven years later, the HIV-infected blood Martha received that day had exploded into full-blown AIDS. "I know that my daughter is dying," Debra acknowledges. "It's especially difficult because Martha is angry. She's very upset that she got the tainted blood and that she's too ill to be like other kids." Martha's faith in God, though, gives her some peace. Debra has also found her own sources of consolation. "I can't cry in front of Martha," Debra says, "but I pray up a storm, and I sing gospel when I'm feeling really heavy. When I'm finished, I still have the same problems, but the singing gives me the strength I need to carry on."

Photograph by Mary Ellen Mark

ABOVE: *In her grandmother's house on the Navajo reservation near Chinle, Arizona, 12-year-old Sha'nah Dawn Harvey receives a ritual shampoo, part of her rite of passage.*

BELOW: *Sha'nah's sister Audrey watches as her grandmother instructs Sha'nah in the techniques of grinding corn, a Navajo symbol of fertility.* Photographs by Paul Chesley

COMING OF AGE

Soon after they begin menstruating, young women on the Navajo Indian reservation near Chinle, Arizona, take part in an elaborate two-day coming-of-age ceremony. Twelve-year-old Sha'nah Dawn Harvey begins the rite of passage with the traditional run in the direction of the rising sun, which Navajos believe is the source of all things. The running is meant to give her the physical and mental strength to enter womanhood. Sha'nah next enters the house of her grandmother, Susie Lee, who privately discloses to her the facts of life and teaches her how to grind corn, a Navajo symbol of fertility. The following morning, before sunrise, relatives wash Sha'nah's hair with suds made from yucca roots that have been harvested by her father. Then, her hair still wet, Sha'nah runs eastward once again at dawn before joining her family in a feast and gift exchange celebrating her womanhood.

CHANGING WOMAN

In Whiteriver, Arizona, Bobbi Jo Lupe is guided into womanhood by elders of the White Mountain Apache tribe. During her four-day coming-of-age ceremony, the most important to the White Mountain Apache people, she symbolically reenacts the story of Changing Woman, or White Painted Woman, the original Apache mother. The rite of passage begins with the exchange of food between the young woman's family and the godparents they have selected for her before the ceremony. Then, assisted by her godmother and the tribal medicine man, the girl dresses in traditional buckskin clothes. An abalone shell is placed on her forehead to protect her against evil, and she wears an eagle feather behind her head so that her spirit will soar to heaven. She is dusted with yellow cattail pollen, a symbol of her fertility and healing powers, and she must pass an endurance test, dancing for hours to symbolically promote the health and welfare of her people. On the last day, her godfather paints her with a sacred mixture of pollen, cornmeal, and ground stones to bless her, and they pass together through a tepee frame made of four poles, symbolizing the four seasons, four directions, and four stages of life.

ABOVE: *Surrounded by family and community members, Bobbi Jo Lupe holds two eagle feathers given to her by her godfather so that her spirit will rise quickly to heaven.*

BELOW: *Bobbi Jo, covered with sacred yellow paint, embraces her mother after completing the strenuous coming-of-age ceremony.*
Photographs by Paul Chesley

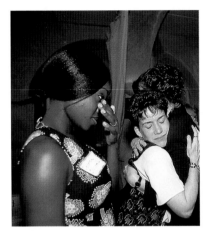

ABOVE AND RIGHT: *Motherless daughters in New York come together to form a "Circle of Remembrance" on the day before Mother's Day.* Photographs by Charlyn Zlotnik

MOTHERS REMEMBERED

On May 11, 1996—the day before Mother's Day—more than 600 women in 17 cities across the country gathered to honor and remember the mothers they had lost. At the same time nationwide, they joined hands in "Circles of Remembrance," in which each woman acknowledged herself and her mother by name. Sponsored by the New York–based group Motherless Daughters, the ceremony brought meaning to a holiday that is often painful for women whose mothers died when they were young. More than 60,000 American girls under age 18 lose their mothers every year. Many suffer from long-lasting feelings of loneliness.

Photographs by Eugene Richards/
Magnum Photos, Inc.

A DAUGHTER LOST

In Houston, Nancy Salem surrounds herself with photographs of her missing daughter, Shafa. She adds her daughter's picture to the bulletin board of the American Association for Lost Children, where images of hundreds of missing children are posted. Since it was founded in 1987, the nonprofit organization has located more than 80 abducted children.

ABOVE: *In her bedroom at home in Valparaiso, Indiana, Kelly Smith shows her mother, Pat, the dress she'll wear for her rehearsal dinner.* Photographs by Dan Dry

SOMETHING TO SMILE ABOUT

For Pat Smith's daughter Kelly, 24, love blossomed over crowns and bridgework. She and her fiancé, Allen Smudde, met as dental students at Northwestern University in Chicago, where they were working together in a treatment clinic. "Kelly has always wanted to be a dentist," Pat relates, "just like her

father, uncle, and grandfather." Despite rain and lightning, Kelly's August wedding came off without a hitch at Our Lady of Loretto Church in Notre Dame, Indiana. Guests then drove an hour to the 120-acre family farm where Kelly and her sister and brother grew up. "It was a little muddy," Pat says, "and I was numb because of everything I had to think about. But it was a beautiful day for her."

ABOVE: *After an emotional ceremony, Pat sits with her daughter for a few minutes while family pictures are taken.*

FOLLOWING PAGES: *Kelly's sister and maid of honor, Shannon, captures a moment during the reception on the family's 120-acre farm.*

ABOVE: *At the Nathaniel Neal Unit, inmate Mary Ann Gomez hugs four of her six children who have traveled from Wyoming to visit her.*
Photographs by Charlyn Zlotnik

HARD TIME

The visiting room at the Nathaniel Neal Unit, a state women's prison in Amarillo, Texas, is large and well lit, with round tables and a cheerful mural of plants and animals. Here, inmates are permitted to visit with their families for up to eight hours a month. Children are allowed into the prison to see their mothers only on Saturdays and Sundays. "It's very emotional," says Vicky Kelly, who brought her twin ten-year-old nieces, Amy and Ashley McElroy, to see their mother, Tammy, for the first time since her incarceration seven months before. "Amy sat on her mom's lap and wouldn't let her go," Vicky explains. "She wanted to glue Tammy's hand to hers so they'd have to stay together. But it was good that the girls saw her. Since Tammy went to prison, they've constantly been saying, 'I wish my mama could see how long my hair is. I wish she could see how big I've gotten.'"

BELOW: *Judy Smith (left) spends time with her daughter Jill on one of her frequent visits.*

ABOVE: *In the prison visiting room, Tammy Yarbrugh holds her twin daughters, Amy (left) and Ashley, for the first time in seven months.*

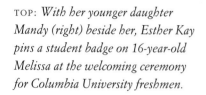

TOP: *With her younger daughter Mandy (right) beside her, Esther Kay pins a student badge on 16-year-old Melissa at the welcoming ceremony for Columbia University freshmen.*

MIDDLE: *Melissa takes in the scene on the university steps.*

BOTTOM: *Farewells become tearful when Melissa (left) gives her mother and sister a good-bye gift—a children's book called* Love You Forever.
Photographs by Nina Barnett

GOING PLACES

Melissa Kay has always loved a challenge. At 16, she chose to enter the freshman class at Columbia University in New York—two years ahead of schedule and clear across the country from her home in Huntington Beach, California. "She's an amazing kid," declares her proud mom, Esther, who single-handedly raised Melissa and her sister, Mandy. Melissa skipped kindergarten and eighth grade, sings Italian arias, and excelled in advanced scientific studies. She's also very strong-willed and determined. "We're a lot alike," Esther remarks, "and had some world-class fights." Despite their occasional head-on collisions, she's quick to point out that she and her daughter are extremely close. "It was gut-wrenching when I left Melissa at school," Esther remembers. "We both did a lot of crying. Back at home, I'd be standing in a supermarket line, and my eyes would well up with tears when I thought about her being away from home. But I'm so proud of her. I know she'll do well."

FROM HAND TO HAND

Amy Healy, 26, was literally wrapped in mother love when she was married at Burntside Lake in Minnesota in September 1996. In the months before, her mother, Jan, had carefully fitted and sewed Amy's wedding dress at the family's summer home in Ferryville, Wisconsin. The gown's iridescent ivory silk had been painstakingly hand-woven by the groom's mother. "Amy is my only daughter," Jan reflects. "It meant so much to me that she wanted me to take part in her wedding in this way." While she was cutting, basting, and finishing the wedding gown, Jan remembers, she spent hours flashing back to Amy's childhood and their years together. "I stitched a lot of love into that dress."

ABOVE: *Amy Healy helps her mother, Jan, cut out the wedding dress pattern they designed together.*

OPPOSITE AND RIGHT: *After Jan checks the fit of the pattern, Amy celebrates with her niece and flower girl, 3-year-old Taylor, while her 81-year-old grandmother looks on.*
Photographs by Judy Griesedieck

Woman to Woman

All women become like their mothers. That is their tragedy. No man does. That's his.

—Oscar Wilde

Oh my god, I sound just like my mother.

—Every woman you've ever met

OPPOSITE:
Faye Cornwell (left) traveled from her home in Oregon to spend two weeks with her daughters, Cherie (center) and Cynthia, and her two granddaughters on Martha's Vineyard, where Cynthia has lived for 12 years. "We all get together at least three times a year," says Cherie, who lives in Washington state. "My sister and my mom are my two best friends in the whole world."
Photograph by Nina Barnett

Photograph by Jeff Jacobson

HARLEY HEAVEN

Jessica Sinclair, age nine, and her mom, Teesa, love watching the action at the week-long biker rally that annually roars through the sleepy town of Sturgis, South Dakota. The two made the 750-mile trip to Sturgis from their home in Idaho on Teesa's Harley, gunning it up to 80 miles an hour on the two-day ride. "I love going fast and feeling the wind blow in my face," says Jessica, who's been riding behind her mom since she was two. "It's kind of scary, but with my mom I feel really safe."

Photograph by Dan Dry

CIRCLE OF FRIENDS

For over 20 years, on the second Tuesday of each month, a group of mothers and daughters has gathered in Indianapolis for a day of sewing and talking that allows them to follow the threads of one another's lives. The Patchwork Guild has been a constant in the life of Cleda Lotze (fourth from right), 85, who started the neighborhood sewing circle with her daughter, Janice Thomas, in 1975. Janice's daughter, Paige (third from right), 27, joined the group when she was six, starting on simple cross-stitching and knitting projects. Other mothers, daughters, and granddaughters have joined over the years, keeping the stitching circle going through good times and bad. Each member of the group, Paige says proudly, has donated material for a quilt she is making. "We learn a lot about crafts from one another," she says, "and a lot about life, too."

ROOTS AND WINGS

In Jackie Young's life, circles overlap—between the personal and political, between her heritage as a Korean-American and her history growing up in Hawaii. For Young, 61, these crossroads are the very places where her life interlaces with those of her three daughters—Paula, 40, Nani, 36, and Laura, 29.

For more than 20 years, their lives have followed very different paths. Paula, her eldest daughter, moved away from home in 1972 when she was 16. A decade later, after Jackie had divorced the girls' father, Laura left at age 15. As years passed and two of the girls grew up far outside her orbit, Jackie gradually transformed herself from a homemaker with a cake-decorating degree into a speech pathologist, an educator with a Ph.D. in communication and women's studies, and a groundbreaking politician—she's the first woman to serve as vice speaker of Hawaii's House of Representatives. Although always close to all of her children, including a son in North Carolina, it was through Jackie's political activity that even stronger ties developed between herself and her three daughters.

She and Paula discovered new common ground—as activists—on Mother's Day 1992. It was shortly after the Los Angeles riots, which had targeted many Korean-American businesses, when Paula, a lawyer, invited Jackie to attend a civil rights commission hearing there. "I was watching my mom speak out to the commission, forcefully expressing a viewpoint that we were all rallying around. I was so proud of her," Paula remembers. Today, Jackie and Paula collaborate frequently as peers on political projects, and Jackie credits her daughter with awakening her interest in her own Korean roots.

RIGHT: *Before heading out for a campaign event, Laura Daniels checks her makeup while her mom, Hawaii State Senate candidate Jackie Young, makes calls.*
Photographs by Lauren Greenfield

Nani, who works in the computer industry, often comes to hear her mother's speeches. And Laura, too, has forged new bonds with her mother as a result of Jackie's political career. After years in San Francisco, Laura has moved to Oahu to live with her mother, serve as treasurer of her campaign, and explore her own Hawaiian heritage. "We lived apart for so long," Laura says. "But now, amazingly, we have a mother-daughter, sister, roommate, best friend, and business relationship."

Jackie believes that the two greatest things you can give your children are roots and wings. And, she adds, that's a gift she and her daughters have given each other—freedom to go their own ways and love enough to come back to one another.

TOP AND ABOVE: *Laura, 29, is Jackie's campaign treasurer and keeps pace with her on a Fourth of July Fun Run/Walk to benefit a local women's shelter.*

On a Kailua roadside, Jackie and Laura "sign wave," a campaign tradition in Hawaii. Jackie's other daughters, Paula, 40, and Nani, 36, have also helped their mom win drive-by votes.

ABOVE: *Reunited after 30 years, Dana Vian (left) gave her birth mother, Joanne Kerr, a jacaranda tree for Mother's Day to symbolize the roots, life, and shelter that they've found together.*

BELOW: *Dana and her mom make up for lost time by living, working, and hanging out together in Encinitas, California.*

Photographs by Cheryl Himmelstein

LOST AND FOUND

Joanne Kerr was 20 years old and unmarried when she gave birth to her daughter, Dana Vian, in Phoenix in 1966. Five days later, she gave the baby girl up for adoption. For the next 30 years, Joanne wondered about the daughter she had lost, and Dana, from the age of four, had an unstoppable determination to find her birth mother. For both of them, luck and longing converged in January 1996. After years of pleading with courts for scraps of information and tracking endless leads, Dana managed to trace her mother.

Since then, the two have been literally inseparable. Dana and her husband, David, left their home in Flagstaff, Arizona, and moved in with Joanne, who owns land in Encinitas, California. Mother and daughter have now started a missing persons business, the Search Company, as well as an advocacy group, the Kerr Heritage Institute, that lobbies for adoption reform. "Dana and I are connected at some deep level that we don't understand very well," says Joanne. "We love animals and green chilis, New Orleans, and Route 66. We both have black-and-white long-haired cats. There are so many similarities and coincidences despite the fact that we were lost to each other for so long." During the years when she was trying to find her mother, Dana remembers fantasizing that they would someday run a business together. "Everything I imagined has come true," she says. "Now that we've come through all this, it's like we've never been apart."

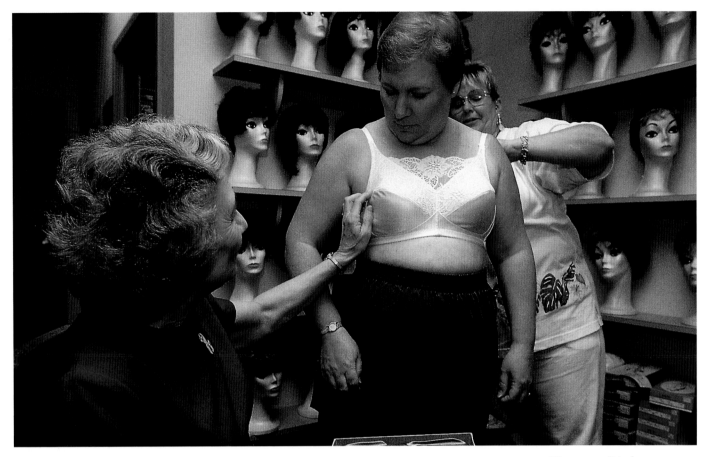

ABOVE: *Charmayne Dierker checks the breast points and fit as her daughter, Lillie Shockney, tries on a new breast prosthesis after cancer surgery.*
Photograph by Annie Griffiths Belt

SURVIVORS' CLUB

When it was time for Lillie Shockney to be fitted for a breast prosthesis in Annapolis, Maryland—seven weeks after her mastectomy for breast cancer—she had no doubt whom she should take along as an advisor. "I brought my mother," Lillie says, "because I knew she'd give me a totally honest, critical view of how I looked. During the fitting, she looked at me just like she did when I was being fitted for my wedding gown. I knew I'd have the best-fitting prosthesis."

Over the past two years, Charmayne Dierker, Lillie's mother, has helped her daughter survive two cancer diagnoses and two mastectomies. The first experience was shattering for Charmayne, who felt responsible for her daughter's illness. "My mother aged ten years during that time," Lillie remembers. The second time around, however, Charmayne knew that Lillie was strong enough to survive, and she had also learned what she could do to help her daughter cope. Since then, the two of them have used their experiences to help hundreds of other mothers and daughters support each other through the trauma of breast cancer. Lillie's book, *The Breast Cancer Survivors' Club*, was published in 1996. And the two of them have cofounded a national nonprofit organization called Mothers Supporting Daughters with Breast Cancer. "Each time we help someone get through this, my mom gets younger," Lillie says.

BRIDGING THE GAP

Barbara Brooks considers herself part of "the sandwich generation." With a 76-year-old mother and a 30-year-old daughter, she often finds herself torn between the two of them and her devotion to her own demanding career. A special education teacher at the inner-city Manual Arts High School in Los Angeles, Barbara, 53, also felt a calling to preach and was recently ordained a deacon in Los Angeles's First African Methodist Episcopal Church. In addition to her heavy church and school responsibilities, Barbara makes herself almost constantly available to her mother, Rosie Harris. "She needs me to go shopping for her, and she likes to talk to me every day, to know everything I'm doing," Barbara says. "She has a way of asking for things without really asking—what I like to call 'mother manipulation.'"

Barbara's daughter, Stephanie, gets a lot of her time and attention as well. An artistic director for a children's theater company, she likes her mother to attend their many performances. Mother and daughter have also been busy planning Stephanie's upcoming wedding. "Stephanie is my heart," Barbara says of her only child. The two of them are so close, she adds, that they each know, when the telephone rings, that it's the other one who's calling.

Although she says it's tough when her mother and daughter need her at the same time, Barbara wouldn't have it any other way. "I'm really stretched between my love for them," she says, "but a lot of people aren't nearly this blessed."

BELOW: *On Mother's Day, Rosie Harris (first row, center) prays with her daughter and granddaughter at the First A.M.E. Church in Los Angeles.*
Photographs by Jan Sonnenmair

*Barbara Brooks (second from left)
counts on her two sisters, Marva
Harris (left) and Tommie Nell Taylor
(far right) to help her look after their
76-year-old mother (center).*

Photograph by Paul Chesley

ANCIENT FOOTSTEPS

Dance, for Roseanne Abrahamson (right), is a living connection to generations past and a physical and spiritual bond with her daughter Dustina, 20 (left). She and Dustina perform traditional Shoshone-Bannock dances frequently and compete in the annual Blackfeet powwow in Browning, Montana, one of the most important events for intertribal dancers in the United States and Canada. "Dance is a form of self-expression, not only for ourselves but for our heritage," says Roseanne, a high school teacher from the Fort Hall Reservation in Idaho. "It is a way to celebrate our history, our culture, and our existence as a people."

RODEO RIVALS

Friendship, trust, and competition have strengthened the bond between Gayla Hawks and her 14-year-old daughter, Jackie. The two of them often ride against each other on the Colorado rodeo circuit, where they star in barrel racing. "Sometimes Jackie beats me, sometimes I beat her," Gayla says. "We're pretty evenly matched."

A single mother, Gayla started racing seriously soon after Jackie was born. When Jackie was nine, she sent a note to her mom letting her know that she wanted to race, too. "She wrote, 'Mom, I want to be a barrel racer and be tough just like you,'" Gayla recalls. "So I got her a horse, and even though she was scared to death at first, she trained him herself. Now Jackie beats most adults she races against. She's a tough competitor."

The two of them spend almost all their time together, practicing and driving their trailer and horses to rodeos as often as five times a week in the summer. It's a lucrative hobby and Jackie, who hopes to go to college and become a veterinarian, plans to buy a pickup truck with her winnings when she turns 17.

ABOVE: *Before she races against her daughter, Jackie, in a rodeo in Fruita, Colorado, Gayla Hawks fixes the 14-year-old's hair, while her nine-year-old son, Tyrell, keeps an eye on the horses.*

FOLLOWING PAGES: *Traveling with and competing against each other on the barrel racing circuit has strengthened Gayla and Jackie's mother-daughter bond.*
Photographs by Paul Chesley

ABOVE AND RIGHT: *Jackie and Gayla don matching rodeo costumes before heading into the arena.*

FOLLOWING PAGES: *Although Jackie had a good run, her mother outmaneuvered her and took first prize in the Fruita barrel race.*

ABOVE: *Elizabeth Little Elk
and her 10-year-old daughter,
Tate Wakan-Win (Holy
Wind Woman), in their
kitchen on South Dakota's
Rosebud Reservation.*
Photographs by Susie Fitzhugh

TIES OF SPIRIT

Elizabeth Little Elk, 46, knew intuitively that she would give birth to a daughter when she became pregnant 10 years ago. "I felt a little afraid of having a
girl," admits Elizabeth, a Sicangu Lakota social worker who lives on the Rosebud
Reservation in South Dakota. "I didn't want her to experience sexism or to be
fearful of the world. And I wanted her to know what it is to be a native woman."
When her daughter was born, Elizabeth's mother, Edna Little Elk, placed her
hand in the baby's mouth, a Lakota tradition that, according to Elizabeth,

breathed her own character and qualities into the child. Edna named her grand-child Tate Wakan-Win (Holy Wind Woman). Ever since, grandmother and grand-daughter have been extraordinarly close. "Tate has slept with my mother in a sin-gle bed since she was two years old," Elizabeth says. "They are very similar in per-sonality. Both of them are artists and very spiritual, strong-willed, compassionate people." Edna, creator of intricate beadwork and quilts, believes that everything one does, even a simple act like walking, should be performed with complete con-sciousness of meaning. Ritual is exceedingly important to her, as it is to her daugh-ter and granddaughter. When Tate was eight, she had her ears ceremonially pierced to signify that she was starting her journey to womanhood. She was also ritually tatooed, another Lakota tradition. "Lakota people believe that when we die, we go through a big open space in the Milky Way called the Spirit Trail," Elizabeth explains. "When the Blue Woman who guards the trail sees Tate's tatoo, she will know she is a Lakota and will let her through."

LEFT: *Edna Little Elk, 80, braids her granddaughter's hair each morning. The two of them have shared a single bed since Tate was two.*

DISTANT SHORES

At 18, Emily MacRae chose to leave the secluded island life of Chappaquiddick Island, Massachusetts, where she had grown up, and headed for Pomona College on the California coast. Her mother, Julia Wells, a reporter for an island weekly, *The Vineyard Gazette,* is philosophical about Emily's decision to move so far away. "She wanted a new life, and she got it," Julia says. "She traded one coast for another, and it's been a great move for her." It was difficult for Julia when her daughter left, but now, after a year of separation, Julia, too, feels that she has moved on. "Being apart feels right for this stage of our relationship," she explains. Electronic mail, they've found, is a great way to bridge the daily distance between them. And when Emily comes home during the summer, they reconnect easily through the many interests that they've always shared—cooking, baseball, playing cards, and harvesting quahogs, the local hardshell clams, in the flats of Katama Bay off Martha's Vineyard. Letting a child go her own way, Julia reflects, "is just one of those gates that you have to go through—and you go through lots of them when your kids are growing up."

RIGHT: *Julia Wells and her daughter,*
Emily MacRae, rake quahogs
in the waters off Martha's Vineyard.
Photograph by Nina Barnett

OVERLEAF: *Mary Jim and her*
daughter, Kerry Schuster, gaze out
over Ice Harbor Dam near Yakima,
Washington, that flooded the lands
of their tribal ancestors when it
was built.
Photograph by Jeff Jacobson

AGING AND RENEWAL

As is the Mother, so is her Daughter.

—EZEKIEL

A MOTHER'S DAY

Once a year, for 20 years, the children, grandchildren, and great-grandchildren of Mary Eldee Collins have gathered to honor her birthday and to celebrate their family. They come from all across the country to the family reunion, which has been held over the years in Kansas, Texas, Colorado, Georgia, and California. They travel in vans and sing joyful gospel songs together. Most of all, they celebrate Eldee, who is now 93. Five feet tall and a country minister's wife in Mexia, Texas, until she was widowed in 1969, Eldee was always there for her eight children, remembers her 57-year-old daughter Rose Miles. "Mama would stay up all night, if needed, to wash our clothes. She had a lot of heads to comb, but she made sure we were always clean and looking right, and at the church door on time. Every day, she had a snack waiting for us when we got home from school. And we could always talk to her and ask for her advice about anything, including sex. She's a wise woman. We remember, and we thank God, that she's still here with us."

Eldee's far-flung family celebrated her most recent birthday in Marina Del Rey, California, where her son now lives. Her 31 grandchildren, 37 great-grandchildren, and three great-great-grandchildren helped her blow out the candles.

ABOVE AND BELOW: *Eldee Collins celebrates her ninety-third birthday in Marina Del Rey, California, with help from her 26 great-granddaughters.*
Photographs by Jan Sonnenmair

Eldee Collins with three generations of her family.

LEFT: *Carole Spotted Eagle cools her 76-year-old mother with a wet towel inside the family tepee.*

RIGHT: *Elaine Sure Chief helps her daughter, Misty Rae New Robe, dress for her dance competition at the Blackfeet powwow.*
Photographs by Paul Chesley

FAMILY DANCE

Every summer, Elaine Sure Chief's family gathers at the Blackfeet powwow held near their home in Browning, Montana. For three days, 12 family members live together in a single tepee, taking part in traditional dance competitions and passing on a sense of tribal heritage to the children. "The kids learn by watching and observing," says Elaine, who works for the Headstart program in Browning. Her nine-year-old daughter, Misty Rae New Robe, has been dancing ever since she could walk and performs in the fast-paced Fancy Shawl Dance competition. "It gives me pride to watch her," Elaine says. "Dancing makes Misty Rae more aware of who she is and her background. I am glad that she is proud to be a Blackfoot."

REACHING BACK

Elly Tally, 85, doesn't often remember who her daughters and grandchildren are. For years, she has suffered from disorientation and confusion. Finally, four years ago, she could no longer take care of herself at home in Denver, Colorado, and her family moved her to Park Manor Nursing Home, also in Denver. "My mother can't tell you what she had for breakfast, but she can describe her childhood perfectly," relates her daughter Caroline Schultz, 59. "Basically, she doesn't know me." Still, Caroline brought her daughter, Sarah Ellis, and two granddaughters—Kelly, 20, and Jessica, 10—to spend a few hours with her mother. "It was a really good day," she says. "She knew my daughter, although she wasn't sure about her great-granddaughters' names. It meant a lot to her to have family there. She remembered."

TOP AND ABOVE: *Caroline Schultz brings her daughter and granddaughters to visit her mother in a Denver nursing home.*
Photographs by Paul Chesley

HARD PARTING

Mary Ann Kreider would do anything for her 85-year-old mother, Theresa Atzinger. "She is just precious to me," says Mary Ann, age 60. For many months she took care of her mother at home in Summerville, South Carolina, with the help of her brother. When their mother's physical condition made this impossible, the three of them made the decision to place Theresa in a nursing home close to Mary Ann. "Mother could see how hard it was getting for me. We talked about it, and she asked me to admit her into a nursing home in Charleston. She's such a strong, wonderful human being. If there was any way that I could keep her with me, I would." Theresa, she says, has adjusted fairly well to her new home. "But it's very hard for me," Mary Ann admits. "I don't know if I ever will get used to it." She calls her mother morning, noon, and night, and visits her nearly every day. Every other weekend, she brings Theresa home for a full day with the family. "Her grandchildren and great-grandchildren adore her," Mary Ann says. "She's so unselfish and has given us all such unconditional love. I know that even if she were unhappy in the home, she wouldn't let us know."

ABOVE AND BELOW: *In a nursing home in Charleston, South Carolina, 85-year-old Theresa Atzinger visits with her daughter, Mary Ann Kreider, and her great-granddaughters Erica, six, and Katie, five.*
Photographs by Susie Post

In Baltimore, Maryland, Charmayne Dierker (right) grieves by the coffin of her 85-year-old mother, Eleanor Shriver, who died after a long, agonizing battle with leukemia. An enormously independent woman—and a perfectionist, Charmayne adds—Eleanor had strapped on her husband's carpentry belt and repaired her own roof at the age of 83. One of the most painful parts of Eleanor's two-year illness, Charmayne says, was the role reversal that took place between them. Eleanor became increasingly frail, requiring that she move into a nursing home, and Charmayne gradually became responsible for dealing with her affairs. "For over three months, I spent three to four hours a day by her side in the nursing home," Charmayne recalls. "It was an extremely difficult time, but my mother taught me the importance of being responsible." Charmayne has also struggled to be strong for her daughter, Lillie Shockney (center), 42, who has suffered through two breast cancer diagnoses and mastectomies since 1992.

FOLLOWING PAGES:

Photograph by Steven Rubin

ABOVE: *In Pasadena, California, Nedra Kirkland, 52, is the primary caregiver for her ailing 74-year-old mother.*
Photographs by Rick Rickman

ALL FOR ONE

Family is everything to Nedra Kirkland, 52, of Pasadena, California. "It's what we start with," she says, "and, in the end, it's the only thing we've got." She and her family have chosen to be as physically close to one another as possible. Nedra lives next door to her 74-year-old mother and two doors down from her brother. Her sister lives around the corner. "There's nothing better than sitting out by the fish pond every morning and having coffee with your mother and brother. It's not something we have to do. It's something we want to do." Her family's unity has been especially important in the months since her mother, Janet Greenup, had surgery for an abdominal aneurism. "I'm her primary caregiver now," Nedra says. "But everybody in the family does their share and more. My brother takes her to all her doctor appointments. My sister gives her emotional support. My niece makes sure her linens are clean and her things are orderly. And my daughter rubs her legs and polishes her nails." Janet's illness has been a difficult adjustment. "My mom used to be a model, and she's always been healthy," Nedra says. "Being so ill has not been easy for her." Nedra, too, has seen her own role change. "I'm now her parent in a lot of ways. I tell her to get dressed when she doesn't want to. I make decisions for her. Sometimes I get tired, but I want to be the one who's there every day, fluffing her pillows. That's what she's always done for me."

Nedra attends to every detail of her mother's comfort. "It's very important to her that her breakfast plate be attractive," Nedra says, "so I spend part of my morning deciding what I'm going to serve her and how to present it."

RIGHT AND OPPOSITE: *In Arizona, tribal elder Susie Lee teaches her granddaughter Audrey Harvey traditional weaving techniques. Sally Sam shows her granddaughter Harriet ancient trails through the steep sandstone walls and cliff-dweller ruins of Canyon de Chelly National Monument on the Navajo reservation.*

Photographs by Paul Chesley

TRACING THE PAST

In northeast Arizona, older Navajo women pass on traditional skills such as weaving and the use of medicinal plants to their daughters and granddaughters to keep knowledge of native practices alive.

FOLLOWING PAGES: *Grandmothers and granddaughters herd sheep by the towering walls of Canyon de Chelly.*

A tribal elder carries the American flag in the ceremonial opening of the Blackfeet powwow in Browning, Montana.
Photograph by Paul Chesley

PHOTOGRAPHERS' BIOGRAPHIES

NINA BARNETT
New York, New York

Nina Barnett is a freelance photographer based in New York City. A graduate of the University of Wisconsin–Madison, Barnett shoots feature and cover assignments for clients such as *Fortune*, *Newsweek*, *Money*, *New York*, *Eating Well*, and *Parade*.

Barnett was the exclusive backstage photographer during the last week of filming for the hit television series *Cheers* and has contributed to numerous book projects, including four Day in the Life books, *The Power to Heal*, and *Jerusalem: In the Shadow of Heaven*. Her work has been exhibited in shows nationwide, most recently in 1996 in *Children of the World: A Woman's Perspective* in New York.

Since 1989, Barnett has been a curator for the William Goldberg Photography Collection in New York. She currently teaches an introductory course in color photography at the NYU School of Continuing Education.

ANNIE GRIFFITHS BELT
Silver Spring, Maryland

Born and raised in Minneapolis, *National Geographic* contract photographer Annie Griffiths Belt earned her Bachelor of Arts in photojournalism from the University of Minnesota. Her professional career began when she was still in school working as a staff photographer for the *Minnesota Daily*. After graduating in 1976, she joined the staff of the award-winning *Worthington Daily Globe* in southern Minnesota.

Griffiths Belt began assignment work for *National Geographic* in 1978. Since then she has worked on dozens of magazine and book projects for the Society, including *National Geographic* stories on Baja California, Israel's Galilee, Britain's Pennine Way, Vancouver, England's Lake District, and Jerusalem. She is currently working on stories for *National Geographic* in the Middle East, Central America, and the United States.

Griffiths Belt's work has also appeared in *Life*, *GEO*, *Smithsonian*, *American Photo*, *Merian*, *Stern*, and many other publications. Her book projects include *Baseball in America*, *The Power to Heal*, *Women in the Material World*, and three Day in the Life books. Her photographs have been exhibited in New York, Washington, Moscow, and Tokyo. She was also the recipient of awards from the National Organization of Women and the White House News Photographers' Association. In addition to her photography, Griffiths Belt lectures and teaches workshops regularly. Her work has also been the subject of a public television documentary.

PAUL CHESLEY
Aspen, Colorado

Paul Chesley is a freelance photographer who has worked with *National Geographic* since 1975. In that time he has completed more than 35 projects for the Society and has traveled extensively through Europe, Asia, and western America.

Chesley's work has been exhibited in museums in New York, London, and Tokyo, and appears regularly in *Time*, *Newsweek*, *GEO*, *Stern*, *Life*, and *Fortune*. He has contributed to 13 Day in the Life books, as well as *Planet Vegas*, *America: Then & Now*, *Bangkok*, *24 Hours in Cyberspace*, *The Circle of Life*, *Seven Days in the Philippines*, *A Passage to Vietnam*, and *The Mission*. Most recently, he was the sole photographer for *The Rockies*, a book produced by *National Geographic*.

DAN DRY
Louisville, Kentucky

Dan Dry is one of America's most decorated photographers, with over 300 national and international photography, advertising, and annual report awards to his credit. In 1981 Dry received the top prize in his field when he was named National Press Photographer by the National Press Photographers' Association. For eight years, Dry traveled the globe on assignment for *National Geographic*. His photographs have appeared in almost every major domestic magazine as well as many foreign publications.

Dry is part of the team that photographed *A Day in the Life of America*, the only photography book in history to top *The New York Times* bestseller list. Dry also shot for *A Day in the Life of Australia*, *A Day in the Life of Japan*, *A Day in the Life of Spain*, and *A Day in the Life of Hawaii*, in which his work graced the book's cover. Dry's photographs have been exhibited in several galleries and museums around the United States, including the National Gallery of Art in Washington, D.C., and the George Eastman House in Rochester, New York. He is also the author of ten books on colleges and universities.

SUSIE FITZHUGH
Seattle, Washington

Susie Fitzhugh began photographing children and families in Baltimore, Maryland, 26 years ago. Since then her work has been displayed in countless group photography shows and four solo exhibitions and appeared in many books and magazines. In the early 1980s, she began a story on western Maryland's Amish community for *Maryland* magazine. This story was later published in both *Life* and *People*.

Fitzhugh has won numerous awards, most recently in 1991 with the Gold First Place Merit Award from the Advertising Club of Western Massachusetts. She has also contributed to the book projects *Raising a Happy Child, Dooryard Garden, Changes Everywhere*, and the multimedia program *Soundings* for the Maryland Arts Folklife Program. Fitzhugh's work is now a part of six permanent collections in Maryland, Washington, and New York.

LAUREN GREENFIELD
Los Angeles, California

Lauren Greenfield is an award-winning documentary photographer affiliated with the Sygma Agency in Paris. Since graduating from Harvard University in 1987, her work has been widely published in magazines such as *The New York Times Magazine, Time, Life, Smithsonian, The London Sunday Times Magazine, Stern*, and *GEO*. Her work has also been exhibited in galleries in New York, Boston, and Los Angeles.

Greenfield was a *National Geographic* intern in 1990, and in 1993 received the first-ever *National Geographic* documentary grant to photograph Los Angeles youth. The resulting work, *Fast Forward: Growing Up in the Shadow of Hollywood*, will be published as a book by Knopf in May 1997 and received the Community Awareness Award in the National Press Photographers' Association Pictures of the Year competition.

In July 1995 Greenfield was featured as one of the five "breakthrough artists" in *American Photo*. Her work has also been honored with grants from the Maine Photographic Workshops, the National Foundation for the Advancement of the Arts, Artists Space, and Radcliffe College. In 1994 she was the director of photography for the Getty Conservation Institute's *Picture L.A.: Landmarks of a New Generation*, an award-winning book and traveling exhibition of photographs by children who documented the landmarks of their communities.

JUDY GRIESEDIECK
Minneapolis, Minnesota

Judy Griesedieck is a freelance photojournalist whose work appears in a variety of publications, including *Time, U.S. News & World Report, Life, People, USA Today*, and *The New York Times*. Griesedieck has worked on numerous Day in the Life projects in China, Italy, and California. Her other book projects include *Baseball in America, Christmas in America, The Power to Heal*, and *The Circle of Life*.

Griesedieck was named Connecticut Photographer of the Year in 1981 and California Photographer of the Year in 1987. In 1988 she was awarded Special Recognition, Canon Photo Essayist, in the Pictures of the Year competition for a project on California's nursing home industry. She has also received numerous awards from the National Press Photographers' Association, including Regional Photographer of the Year in 1989.

CHERYL HIMMELSTEIN
Pasadena, California

Born in Tucson, Arizona, Cheryl Himmelstein's focus as an undergraduate changed from fine arts to photography while working as a photo researcher for Black Star Publishing in New York. She then moved to Pasadena to study at the Art Center College of Design and graduated in 1995 with a bachelor of fine arts degree in photography. Her freelance career began while she was in school as a stringer for the *Pasadena Star News*, and her work has since appeared in such publications as *Guitar Player, Option, Parenting, San Francisco Focus, Der Speigel, Time*, and *Westways*. Himmelstein also works regularly with universities, newspapers, and commercial clients. Her work is currently on file with photo agencies in New York, California, and Arizona.

JEFF JACOBSON
Topanga, California

After a brief career in law, Jeff Jacobson changed his course to pursue photography. He is now an award-winning photojournalist whose accomplishments include contributions to numerous books, such as *My Fellow Americans, Mexico Through Foreign Eyes, Eyes of Time, Flesh and Blood: Photographers' Images of Their Own Families*, and *Photojournalism in America*. His work has appeared in many publications, including *Aperture, Life, The New York Times Magazine, Rolling Stone, Art in America, GEO, Entertainment Weekly*, and *Fortune*.

Jacobson's photographs have been exhibited worldwide. In 1988 he was given a grant in photography from the New York Foundation for the Arts, and was honored in 1990 with an NEA Fellowship in photography. He is currently a faculty member at the International Center of Photography in New York City, where he conducts biannual workshops.

BARBARA LAING
Midland, Texas

A photojournalist for 18 years, Laing's credits include publication in *The New York Times Magazine, National Geographic, Audubon, Life, Sports Illustrated, Stern, Newsweek, Texas Monthly*, and *Fortune*. She has also worked extensively for corporate clients, including U.S. Steel, Frito Lay, and Microsoft.

Laing studied photography at the San Francisco Art Institute for two years before going on to win Best News Picture in the 1981 Pictures of the Year competition sponsored by the National Press Photographers' Association/University of Missouri. In 1984 her work for the *Dallas Times Herald* made her the NPPA Texas Photographer of the Year. In 1993 Laing's photography was exhibited in a show entitled In Praise of Women Photographers, produced by Time Warner.

Over the past two years, Laing has covered the Oklahoma City bombing, the Unabomber arrest, toxic-waste dumping in Texas, and Olympic athletes in training. She currently lives in Midland, Texas, with her husband and children, Maryemma and Henry.

MARY ELLEN MARK
New York, New York

Mary Ellen Mark has achieved worldwide visibility through her numerous photo essays and portraits in such magazines as *The New Yorker*, *Life*, *The New York Times Magazine*, *Harper's Bazaar*, *Stern*, *Details*, *Allure*, *Rolling Stone*, and *The London Sunday Times Magazine*. For over two and a half decades she has traveled extensively on professional assignments making pictures that reflect a high degree of humanism. Her portrayal of Mother Teresa was the product of many years of work in India, and a photographic essay on runaway children in Seattle became the basis of the Academy Award–nominated film *Streetwise*, directed and photographed by her husband, Martin Bell.

In 1994 Mary Ellen Mark was awarded a John Guggenheim Fellowship, the Matrix Award for outstanding woman photographer, and the Dr. Erich Salomon Award for outstanding merits in the field of photojournalism. She was also presented with honorary doctor of fine arts degrees from her alma mater, the University of Pennsylvania, as well as from the University of the Arts. She has published 11 books, including *Mother Teresa's Mission of Charity in Calcutta*, *The Photo Essay: Photographers at Work*, *Streetwise*, *Mary Ellen Mark: Twenty-five Years*, and most recently, *A Cry for Help*. Mark's photographs have been exhibited worldwide, and a retrospective, Mary Ellen Mark: Twenty-five Years, is currently on an international tour.

SUSIE POST
Pittsburgh, Pennsylvania

Susie Post is a freelance photographer with a passion for documenting life in diverse communities. From coverage of the Anabaptist Hutterites and the Aran Islands in Ireland to that of a high school in middle-America, her work spans a range of cultures. In the past six years, Post has contributed the majority of her work to *National Geographic* and *Missions USA*, documenting the stories of people living with AIDS and the people who help them. The resulting material was compiled into the educational series, *Salt in Their Tears*.

Post has been the recipient of numerous awards, including the Robert F. Kennedy Award for coverage of the disadvantaged and individual portrait and news awards in POY. Her work has appeared in *The New York Times Magazine*, *World Vision*, *Compassion International*, and *Food for the Hungry*. She has also traveled through various regions of the world, including Africa, Europe, and South America. Before her freelance career, Post was a staff photographer at *The Pittsburgh Press* and *The Morning News Tribune* in Tacoma, Washington. She has also taught at the Mountain Workshop, the Missouri Workshop, and the University of the Nations in Hawaii.

RICK RICKMAN
Laguna Niguel, California

Rick Rickman's photography has taken him around the world to shoot people, cultures, and important world events. A graduate of New Mexico State, he garnered international recognition in 1985 after winning the Pulitzer Prize for news photography.

Rickman's images have appeared in *National Geographic*, *Life*, *Time*, *GEO*, *People*, *Audubon*, and other publications. His work is represented by Matrix International, a world renowned photography agency, and has been used by numerous major corporations.

Rickman's photographs have been exhibited internationally as part of traveling shows for the Smithsonian Institute, and in Germany and Japan at major expos. He has been featured on PBS and has lectured at photography workshops and corporate seminars. Rickman's work has also appeared in numerous books, including *Christmas Around the World*, *The Power of Healing*, *Baseball in America*, and four books in the Day in the Life series. His work was also featured on the cover of *Pursuit of Ideas*.

STEVEN RUBIN
Baltimore, Maryland

Steven Rubin received his academic training in sociology. His undergraduate fieldwork among gypsies led him to pursue documentary photography, through which he felt the concerns of sociology could be powerfully communicated. In 1994 Rubin was selected for an Alicia Patterson Foundation Fellowship, which allowed him to continue his long-term photo essay *Poverty in Vacationland: Life in a Backwoods Maine Community*. Rubin was honored with a New York Foundation for the Arts Photography Fellowship, an Award of Excellence from the National Press Photographers' Association, and the Leica Medal of Excellence.

Rubin's work has appeared in *The New York Times Magazine*, *Time*, *Newsweek*, *Fortune*, *The Village Voice*, *The Independent Magazine*, *Stern*, *GEO*, and *L'Express*. His participation in book projects has included *A Day in the Life of Thailand*, *A Day in the Life of Israel*, and *Jerusalem: In the Shadow of Heaven*.

JOEL SARTORE
Lincoln, Nebraska

Raised in the town of Ralston, Nebraska, Joel Sartore attended the University of Nebraska at Lincoln, where he received a degree in journalism. After college, he worked for six years at the *Wichita Eagle* (Kansas), first as a photographer, then as director of photography. Sartore has been a contract photographer for *National Geographic* since 1992. During this time he has covered the American West extensively, focusing on land-use issues, ecosystems, and endangered species.

Sartore was a Pulitzer Prize finalist in 1986, Photographer of the Year for the National Press Photographers' Association Region 7 in 1986, and won the Award of Excellence in the 1992 POY competition for Magazine Photographer of the Year. He was also a speaker on the NPPA Flying Short course in the fall of 1993.

MICHAEL A. SCHWARZ
Atlanta, Georgia

Michael A. Schwarz is a freelance corporate, editorial, and documentary photojournalist. His work is published internationally and has appeared in *Fortune, The Chronicle of Higher Education, Business Week, U.S. News & World Report, National Geographic Traveler*, and *USA Today*. He has received a number of awards from the Pictures of the Year competition, and won the Dag Hammarskjold Award for Human Rights Advocacy Journalism. Schwarz is a Baltimore native and a graduate of the Rochester Institute of Technology. He is co-chairman of the Atlanta Photojournalism Seminar and hosts the monthly First Tuesday Photojournalism Chat on the Internet. His work can be found at http://www.mindspring.com/~atlphoto/schwarz.html.

JAN SONNENMAIR
Los Angeles, California

Jan Sonnenmair is a freelance photojournalist whose work has been published extensively in magazines such as *People, Life, Newsweek, Time, Modern Maturity, Sports Illustrated*, and *Business Week*. She recently finished work on a collaborative project addressing the multifaceted issue of children with AIDS. The project was published in *Life* and won the 1993 Budapest Award for photo essay from the World Press Foundation. Her other past projects have included coverage of the 1986 Philippines presidential campaign, the 1988 summer

Olympics, poverty on the Texas/Mexico border, indigent health care, and the story of a young mother raising her autistic son.

Formerly a staff photographer at the *Dallas Morning News*, Sonnenmair has been the recipient of numerous awards, including the Texas Headliners 1st Place Award for Photography, the Society of Newspaper Designers Award of Merit, and the William Randolph Hearst Foundation Photography Award.

SCOTT THODE
New York, New York

Scott Thode is an award-winning photographer whose work has appeared in *The New York Times Magazine, Life, Stern, GEO, Paris Match*, and many other North American and European publications. In 1985 Thode began *Bailey House: Riding the AIDS Rollercoaster*, a photographic essay about the only residence in New York City for homeless people with AIDS. He has spent much of the last eight years documenting the day-to-day struggle of one HIV-afflicted person, and will soon publish his book *The Spirit Within*, a series of portraits and writings by people who are HIV-positive or have AIDS.

Thode's work has been exhibited at the Visage Pour L'Image photo festival in Perpignon, France, in the Electric Blanket AIDS Project, at the Colonnade Gallery in Washington, D.C., and at the P.S. 122 Gallery in New York City.

CHARLYN ZLOTNIK
New York, New York

Charlyn Zlotnik is a freelance photographer based in New York City. Her international career has led her to cover stories in the Philippines, India, South Korea, Burma, Vietnam, Panama, and Cuba. Her work has ranged from stories on the Palm Springs Follies to Bedford Hills Prison, and includes long-term coverage of country and western singer Willie Nelson.

Zlotnik's work has appeared in *The New York Times, Newsweek, Time, Life, Business Week*, and many other books and publications. Her photographs appear in a traveling exhibition by Time Warner called *It's Us—A Celebration of Who We Are in America Today*.

ACKNOWLEDGMENTS

Project Staff:

EDITORS
Jain Lemos
Elizabeth Viscott Sullivan
Patricia Levi

DIRECTOR OF PHOTOGRAPHY
Peter Howe

TEXT
Susan Wels

PROJECT COORDINATOR
Gwendolyn Wynne

ASSIGNMENT RESEARCHERS
Kelley Bass
Pamela Tom
Colleen Wilson
Gwendolyn Wynne

ART DIRECTOR
Renato Stanisic

DESIGN
BTD / Beth Tondreau

Special thanks to:

The entire documentary team of *The Story of Mothers &
Daughters*, the countless mothers and daughters who shared
their extraordinary lives and stories with us, and the following
individuals: Wilhelmina Adams, Judy and Reagan Armstrong,
Tim Atzinger, Bob Bell, Dorice Beren, Carole Bidnick, Barbara
Brooks, Don Cannalte, Lynn, Alverna, and Cai Cody, Wayne
Cody, Valerie Crews, Paula Daniels, Dr. Kay S. Daugherty,
Motherless Daughters, Charmayne S. Dierker, Bonnie Dittman,
Aaron Donnelly, Marissa Donnelly, Patricia Donnelly,
Victoriana Donnelly, Tom Dunlop, Hope Edelman, Gail
Eisenberg, Kellie Ellis, Sarah Ellis and Family, Judy Flood,
Sister Francine, Ken Fund, Sue Garcia, Melissa Germaine,
Ericka and Jerry Gloshay, Jerry Gloshay Sr., Janet Greenup,
Marta Hallett, Stacy Halper, Amelia Hart, Sha'nah Dawn
Harvey, Suzanne and Anderson Harvey and Family, Gayla and
Jackie Hawks and Family, Jone Jackson, Robin and Ron
Johnson and Family, Terry Jordan, Babbs Kaplinsky, Esther
Kay, Melissa Kay, Joanne Kerr, Nedra Kirkland, Sarah Krall,
Wendy Leonard, Susie Lee, Renata and Bobbi Jo Lupe and
Family, Chairman Ronnie Lupe, Allison Martin, Stephanie
McCormick-Goodhart, Maureen McFadden, Julia Mitchell,
Hugh and Eleanor Monroe and Family, Joseph Montebello,
Samantha Moss, *Native Peoples Magazine*, Mona and Adam
Nordwall and Family, Chief Earl Old Person, Kate O'Neal,
Soleil O'Neal Sullivan, Sally Price Sam, Ramona, Norman, and
Shannon Roach, Harriet and Tom Joe Sam, Pete Sheehan, Lillie
D. Shockney, Pat and Hugh Smith, Al Smudde, Kelly Smudde,
Carol and Molly Spotted Eagle and Family, Harvey Sure Chief
and Family, Amy Swarr, Deanne Jean Tah, Ida P. Tah, Nathaniel
Neal Unit and Staff, University Hospital–Denver, Dana Vian,
Carole Vandermeyde, Mickey Wadolny, and Jackie Young.